GENERATIVE ARTIFICIAL INTELLIGENCE FOR BEGINNERS

Unravel the Mysteries of AI With Ease and Confidence Through Practical Guides, Ethical Insights, and Real-World Applications

---

GWEN TAYLOR

© **Copyright Gwen Taylor 2024 - All rights reserved.**

The content within this book may not be reproduced, duplicated or transmitted without direct written permission from the author or the publisher.

Under no circumstances will any blame or legal responsibility be held against the publisher or author for any damages, reparation, or monetary loss due to the information contained within this book. Either directly or indirectly. You are responsible for your own choices, actions, and results.

Legal Notice:

This book is copyright-protected and only for personal use. You cannot amend, distribute, sell, use, quote, or paraphrase any part of the content without the consent of the author or publisher.

Disclaimer Notice:

Please note that the information in this document is for educational and entertainment purposes only. All effort has been expended to present accurate, up-to-date, reliable, and complete information. No warranties of any kind are declared or implied. Readers acknowledge that the author does not render legal, financial, medical, or professional advice. The content within this book has been derived from various sources. Please consult a licensed professional before attempting any techniques outlined in this book.

By reading this document, the reader agrees that the author is under no circumstances responsible for any direct or indirect losses incurred from using the information contained within this document, including, but not limited to, errors, omissions, or inaccuracies.

Contents

Introduction ... 7

1. WHAT IS GENERATIVE AI? ... 9
   The Evolution of AI to Generative Models ... 9
   Defining Generative AI: Beyond the Buzzword ... 12
   How Generative AI Works: A Simplified Overview ... 14
   The Distinction Between AI and Generative AI ... 16
   Generative AI's Place in Today's Tech Landscape ... 19

2. UNLOCKING THE BRAIN OF AI ... 23
   Neural Networks: The Brain Behind AI ... 23
   Algorithms: The Instructions AI Follows ... 26
   Data: The Fuel of Generative AI ... 28
   Machine Learning vs. Deep Learning in Generative AI ... 31
   Key Technologies Powering Generative AI ... 34

3. TAILORING YOUR WORLD WITH GENERATIVE AI ... 39
   Smart Homes and AI: A Practical Utopia ... 42
   Enhancing Creativity in Art and Music ... 45
   Generative AI in Personal Health and Fitness ... 48
   AI-Enhanced Educational Tools ... 51

4. THE NEW FRONTIERS OF CUSTOMER EXPERIENCE ... 57
   Streamlining Operations and Manufacturing ... 60
   AI in Marketing: Personalization at Scale ... 63
   Financial Forecasting and Risk Management ... 66
   The Role of AI in Sustainable Practices ... 69

5. NAVIGATING THE ETHICAL MAZE OF
   GENERATIVE AI ... 73
   Bias and Fairness in AI Algorithms ... 73
   Privacy Concerns in the Age of AI ... 76
   Ethical Design and Development Practices ... 79
   The Future of Employment and AI ... 82
   Regulation and Governance of AI Technologies ... 85

6. AI AND THE FUTURE OF TOMORROW ... 93
   AI's Role in Shaping Future Societies ... 93
   Visual Element: Infographic on AI in Daily Life ... 95
   Interactive Element: AI Readiness Quiz ... 96
   Creativity and AI: Collaboration or Competition? ... 97
   The Digital Divide and Access to AI ... 99
   AI and Its Impact on Privacy and Security ... 103
   Preparing for an AI-Enhanced Future ... 106

7. UNLOCKING GENERATIVE AI TOOLS FOR
   EVERYONE ... 111
   Step-by-Step Guide to Using ChatGPT ... 114
   Exploring Creative AI with DALL-E ... 116
   Unveiling Google's Gemini (formerly Bard) ... 119
   AI Tools for Writers and Content Creators ... 121
   Building Your First AI Project ... 124

8. THE AI LEARNING CURVE: RESOURCES TO
   GET YOU GOING ... 127
   Online Courses and Resources for AI Learning ... 127
   Community and Forum Engagement for AI
   Enthusiasts ... 130
   Challenges and Competitions to Sharpen Your AI
   Skills ... 133
   The Importance of a Growth Mindset in AI
   Learning ... 136
   Future-Proofing Your Career with AI Skills ... 138

9. THE FRONTIER OF GENERATIVE AI: TODAY'S RESEARCH, TOMORROW'S REALITY — 143
AI in Space Exploration and Environmental Science — 146
The Next Frontier: AI in Quantum Computing — 149
Ethical AI: Toward More Responsible Innovations — 153
Predicting the Unpredictable: AI's Role in Future Predictions — 156

10. RIDING THE WAVE: ADAPTING TO AI'S EVOLUTION — 161
Visual Element: AI Skills Infographic — 163
Interactive Element: AI Readiness Quiz — 164
The Role of Education in an AI-Enhanced World — 164
Ethical Considerations for Future AI Innovations — 167
Community and Societal Engagement with AI — 170
Embracing AI: A Call to Action for Everyone — 173

Afterword — 177
Bibliography — 183

Introduction

The world is on the brink of something monumental, a shift so significant that it's like the dawn of the internet all over again. Still, this time, it's the AI revolution. Generative AI is at the forefront, leading the charge with its ability to create, innovate, and solve problems in ways we've only dreamed of. From revolutionizing healthcare with personalized treatment plans to transforming creative industries with AI-generated art, the potential is boundless. And guess what? You're holding the ticket to ride this wave of change.

Hey there! I'm your guide on this exciting journey. Not too long ago, I was just like you, curious yet bewildered by the world of AI. But as I dove deeper, my apprehension turned into fascination, and before I knew it, AI became my passion. I've made it my mission to pull back the curtain on AI, making it accessible and understandable for everyone, regardless of their technical savvy. I believe in the power of AI to enrich our lives, and I'm committed to helping you discover that power for yourself.

I know what you might think: "But isn't AI going to steal our jobs and make humans obsolete?" Let's tackle those fears head-on. While it's true that AI will change the way we work, it's more about augmentation than replacement. Imagine having a supersmart assistant who can handle the tedious tasks, leaving you free to focus on what humans do best—creativity, empathy, and innovation. That's what AI promises in the future, which we should embrace with open arms.

This book is your beginner-friendly guide to navigating the world of generative AI. We will start with the basics, demystifying the jargon and breaking down complex concepts into bite-sized, digestible pieces. From there, we'll explore the practical applications of AI, the ethical considerations we must keep in mind, and the exciting possibilities that lie ahead. Each section is designed to build on the last, ensuring you walk away with a solid understanding of what AI is and how you can harness its potential.

But this isn't just a book to read; it's a book to do. Along the way, I'll provide practical steps, tools, and projects to try out for yourself because the best way to learn is by doing. By the end of this book, you won't just understand AI—you'll be able to apply it in your own life and work.

So, I invite you to approach this book with an open mind and a healthy curiosity. Let's embark on this adventure together as passive observers and active participants in shaping an AI-driven future.

And remember, the journey into the world of AI isn't reserved for the tech elite; it's for anyone with a passion for learning and a desire to make a difference. Together, we can demystify AI and unlock its potential to transform our world. Let's get started, shall we?

ONE

What is Generative AI?

Diving into the ocean of generative AI, it's not the depth that astounds us but the life it harbors, evolving from the simplest forms to creatures of complexity and wonder. This evolution mirrors the journey of artificial intelligence (AI), which has grown from basic, rule-based algorithms to today's generative models capable of creating content that feels almost human. Technological progress and a fundamental shift in how we perceive and harness AI's capabilities are at the heart of this transformation.

The Evolution of AI to Generative Models

In the early days, AI was like a newborn, figuring out human intelligence through basic, rule-based systems. These systems were groundbreaking then but relied heavily on predefined human-set rules. They could perform specific tasks like playing chess or solving math problems but couldn't learn or create beyond their programming. It was a time full of potential, suggesting a future where machines might mimic human thought processes.

Historical Milestones

The journey from these early days to today's advanced generative models has seen many important milestones. The introduction of machine learning in the late 20th century was a key turning point, moving AI from static rule-based systems to dynamic models that could learn from data. This change was huge, allowing AI to adapt and improve, and it set the stage for even more advanced AI models.

Technological Advancements

Key technological breakthroughs have been instrumental in this evolution. The development of neural networks, inspired by the human brain's structure, introduced a new paradigm for AI. These networks, composed of layers of interconnected nodes, could process and interpret complex patterns in data, from recognizing faces in photos to understanding natural language. Introducing deep learning, a subset of machine learning involving deeper neural networks, further accelerated AI's capabilities, enabling it to tackle increasingly complex and nuanced tasks.

Shift in Paradigms

This technological progress sparked a significant shift in the focus of AI research. The ambition expanded from creating AI that could analyze and interpret data to developing models to generate entirely new data. Generative AI emerged from this ambition, significantly departing from the limitations of traditional AI. Instead of merely recognizing patterns, generative models could create new images, write text, and compose music, blurring the lines between machine-generated and human-created content.

For instance, consider the task of designing a new product. In the past, AI could assist by analyzing market trends and suggesting features based on what has worked before. With generative AI, the approach is radically different. It can now produce innovative design prototypes, simulate consumer reactions to other designs, and even predict market trends, all by learning from existing data and generating new, unseen concepts.

Impact on Industries

The implications of this shift are profound, touching every corner of our lives. In the arts, generative AI creates new forms of expression, from AI-painted artworks that fetch thousands at auctions to music albums where the composer is an algorithm. In healthcare, AI models generate synthetic data for research, preserving patient privacy while providing valuable insights into diseases and treatments. Engineers use AI to design more efficient engines, and architects use AI to envision buildings that blend form and function in novel ways.

The common thread in these examples is AI's ability to generate new solutions, ideas, and creations, pushing the boundaries of what's possible. This evolution from simple, rule-based AI to today's generative models represents a leap in technological capability and our approach to problem-solving and creation. It's a testament to human ingenuity and a glimpse into a future where AI and human creativity converge, opening up limitless possibilities.

As we explore the depths of generative AI, it's clear this is just the beginning. With each technological breakthrough, we're not just building more intelligent machines but reshaping the landscape of innovation, creativity, and discovery. The journey of AI, from its rule-based infancy to the generative powerhouses of today, is a narrative of progress and potential. In this narrative, the next chapter is ours to write.

Defining Generative AI: Beyond the Buzzword

Generative AI is impressive in tech because it can understand and process data and create new things. Instead of just following instructions, it can create original content like text, images, music, and more. It goes beyond traditional AI by adding new creations to the mix.

Clarifying Definitions

Generative AI is about creating new data outputs based on the data it has been trained on. It doesn't just copy or mimic; it uses what it has learned to produce original content. This makes it different from other types of AI that focus on decision-making or pattern recognition.

Types of Generative AI

Two popular frameworks illustrate the diversity within generative AI:

- GANs (Generative Adversarial Networks): Think of GANs as a pair of artists in a constant critique session. One creates, and the other evaluates. The creator or generator produces images, while the evaluator or discriminator judges them against authentic images. This back-and-forth continues until the creations are indistinguishable from actual photos. This method has been a game-changer in creating realistic images and deepfakes.
- VAEs (Variational Autoencoders): VAEs are like conceptual artists, focusing on understanding the essence of their subjects. They learn to encode data into a compressed form and then decode it to generate new data. This process is critical for tasks where capturing the

underlying structure of data is crucial, such as in voice synthesis or style transfer in art.

Applications

The applications of generative AI are as varied as they are fascinating:

- Art and design AI now produces artwork hanging in galleries alongside human-made pieces. It's also used in fashion to design new garments.
- Filmmakers use generative AI for special effects, and game developers create expansive, dynamic worlds.
- Healthcare benefits from generative models that can simulate medical data for research, improving patient outcomes without compromising privacy.
- Business applications include generating realistic product mockups and creating content for marketing campaigns.

The versatility of generative AI is a testament to its transformative potential across sectors.

Potential Misconceptions

Despite its promise, some misconceptions about generative AI need clearing up:

- It's not about replacing human creativity. Instead, it's a tool that enhances and extends our creative capabilities, offering new ways to express ideas.
- Generative AI doesn't "understand" what it creates in the way humans do. It recognizes patterns and learns from data but lacks consciousness or intent.

- Not all output is gold. Just as a novice painter might produce a masterpiece or a mess, generative AI creations sometimes require human intervention to reach their full potential.

Understanding these nuances is crucial for appreciating generative AI's value and potential.

How Generative AI Works: A Simplified Overview

Peeling back the layers of generative AI might seem daunting at first glance, but let's simplify it, stripping away the techspeak to get to the heart of how these marvels operate. It's less about wires and codes and more about teaching a system to tap into its inner artist or inventor, albeit with a digital twist.

Basic Principles

Generative AI is about learning from examples. It looks at a lot of data, finds patterns and structures, and then uses that knowledge to create new data similar to the original. The key is the AI's ability to understand and replicate the complex relationships within the data it analyzes.

Training Process

The training of a generative AI model is similar to an apprenticeship. The model starts with no knowledge and gradually learns through exposure to examples. This learning phase involves several steps:

- Data Collection: The first step is gathering a dataset from which the AI will learn. This dataset could be anything from pictures of dogs to music segments, depending on what the AI is meant to generate.

- Model Adjustment: As the AI reviews the data, it makes numerous small adjustments to its internal settings, similar to tuning a musical instrument to get the perfect sound. These settings govern how the AI interprets and processes information.
- Feedback Loop: The AI's creations are compared to the original data throughout the training. It's a process of trial and error, where the model learns from its mistakes and successes to improve its output.

Input to Output

Give a seasoned poet a theme for a new poem. They take this theme, draw upon their years of reading and writing poetry, and craft a new piece. Generative AI works under a similar principle. It takes an input, such as a prompt or a base image, processes it through the lens of what it has learned during training, and produces an original piece of content. This output is the AI's "response" to the input, informed by the patterns and structures it has uncovered in its training data.

For example, if you give a generative AI model trained on landscape paintings a description like "a snowy mountain under a starry night," it doesn't just find a similar image in its database. Instead, it uses its knowledge of snow, mountains, and starry nights from its training to create a brand new image.

Real-Life Analogies

To further demystify how generative AI operates, look at a couple of real-life analogies:

- Cooking from Scratch: Imagine you've been learning to cook by following various cuisines. Over time, you start experimenting, mixing ingredients and techniques you've

learned to create a dish that's entirely your own. That's similar to how generative AI works, combining elements it has learned from data to cook up something new.
- Writing a Novel: A novelist who has read a lot of different genres needs to copy what they've read. Instead, they use their reading experience to create new stories. In the same way, generative AI, after learning from data, creates original content that feels familiar.

These analogies underscore a crucial point about generative AI: it's about synthesis, not replication. The AI takes its broad "experiences" of data, mixes them in novel ways, and produces something original yet grounded in what it has learned. This capability makes generative AI an exciting technological frontier, offering a glimpse into a future where machines can complement human creativity and offer us new ways to imagine and innovate.

The Distinction Between AI and Generative AI

To grasp the essence of generative AI, it's pivotal to differentiate it from the broader umbrella it resides in artificial intelligence (AI) itself. In its broadest sense, AI is the simulation of human intelligence in machines. These machines are designed to mimic human actions, whether solving complex equations or recognizing speech. Traditional AI systems are adept at analyzing vast datasets, identifying patterns, and making decisions based on predefined rules or learned information.

Defining AI

Traditional AI operates across various functionalities, from simple tasks like sorting emails based on content to more complex operations such as navigating vehicles autonomously. Its mainstay is analyzing and learning from data to perform tasks that typically require human intelligence, such as understanding languages or recognizing objects in images. These capabilities make traditional AI invaluable in fields where decision-making is based on data analysis, including finance, healthcare diagnostics, and customer service.

Generative vs. Analytical

While traditional AI focuses on understanding and interpreting data, generative AI leaps forward. It uses its learned knowledge to create new, original content that didn't exist before. This distinction is like the difference between someone who can critique art based on what they've learned and an artist who creates new pieces inspired by their knowledge and experiences. Generative AI, therefore, is not just reactive (analyzing and responding to data) but proactive, bringing new creations into existence.

Scope of Creativity

The introduction of generative AI expands the horizon of creativity and innovation, transcending traditional boundaries. Previously, AI's role in creative tasks was primarily limited to providing insights or enhancing human-created content. Now, with generative capabilities, AI is a creator in its own right, producing artworks, music, and literature that resonate with human emotions and aesthetics. This shift doesn't diminish the value of human creativity. Still, it enriches it, offering tools that augment our ability to innovate and express ourselves. For instance, designers can use generative AI to explore new fashion trends, architects can visualize buildings that blend with their environment in unprecedented ways, and writers can find inspiration for plots or characters.

Future Implications

The distinction between traditional and generative AI is more than academic; it has profound implications for the future of technology and society. As generative AI continues to evolve, its potential applications seem boundless. In medicine, it could lead to the creation of personalized treatment plans generated from a patient's unique data profile. In environmental science, it might produce models to predict climate change impacts more accurately. The creative industries could see a renaissance, with AI partnering with humans to create works of art and literature that push the boundaries of imagination.

However, this burgeoning capability also prompts essential ethical and practical questions. As AI creates content, copyright, originality, and authenticity issues emerge. The role of AI in shaping opinions and generating information, especially in sensitive areas like news and politics, will require careful consideration and regulation.

Moreover, the democratization of creativity through AI opens up opportunities for individuals and communities who have historically been marginalized in creative industries. With tools that lower the barriers to entry, a wider diversity of voices and perspectives can be heard, enriching the global cultural fabric.

Therefore, the distinction between AI and generative AI is not merely one of capability but of philosophy and approach. Traditional AI helps us understand the world as it is, while generative AI empowers us to imagine the world as it could be. This shift from analytical to creative, reactive to proactive, marks a pivotal moment in our technological evolution, promising a future where AI solves problems and inspires us to see beyond the horizon.

Generative AI's Place in Today's Tech Landscape

Generative AI has swiftly moved from the margins to the mainstream of the technology landscape, quietly infiltrating various sectors and embedding itself in the fabric of daily digital experiences. From the art pieces that challenge our perceptions of creativity to the personalized media content that seems to know our preferences better than we do ourselves, generative AI applications are as diverse as they are transformative.

Current Applications

The reach of generative AI extends across multiple domains, demonstrating its versatility and wide-ranging utility. In content creation, for instance, marketing teams leverage AI to craft copy that resonates with targeted demographics, tailoring messages with a precision that manual analysis could hardly achieve. Meanwhile, entertainment platforms use generative algorithms to recommend movies and shows, creating a personalized viewing experience that keeps users engaged and subscribed.

In the art world, generative AI challenges traditional notions of creativity, producing works that have found their place in galleries and private collections. These AI-created pieces, with their complex patterns and textures, often leave viewers pondering the nature of art itself. Healthcare sees generative AI modeling protein structures as a task that could lead to groundbreaking medical treatments and was once thought to be beyond the reach of computational methods.

Innovation and Disruption

By pushing the boundaries of what's possible, generative AI acts as a catalyst for innovation, reshaping industries from the ground up. The fashion industry, for instance, now experiments with AI-driven designs, merging data from past trends with generative models to forecast and even shape future styles. In architecture, generative AI assists in creating structures that optimize space, light, and materials in previously unimaginable ways, disrupting traditional design processes.

This disruption is not without its tensions. Traditional roles and industries find themselves at a crossroads where adaptation is beneficial and necessary to stay relevant. The publishing industry grapples with AI-generated literature, exploring new models of authorship and copyright. Retail sees generative AI transforming inventory management and customer service, challenging businesses to integrate these technologies or risk obsolescence.

Ethical and Social Considerations

With great power comes great responsibility, and the deployment of generative AI is fraught with ethical dilemmas and social implications. One pressing concern is the potential for misinformation as AI increasingly generates realistic images, videos, and texts indistinguishable from authentic content. The specter of deepfakes looms large, necessitating rigorous verification methods and ethical guidelines.

Bias in AI remains a stubborn issue, reflecting prejudices present in the data sets used for training. Without careful oversight, AI could amplify societal inequalities rather than alleviate them. The conversation around AI and employment also intensifies, with debates focusing on the balance between technological advancement and job displacement. Ensuring that the benefits of AI are equitably distributed requires thoughtful policy and inclusive dialogue.

Future Trends

Peering into the future of generative AI, several trends suggest exciting and, in some cases, challenging times ahead. Interactivity and collaboration between AI and humans are set to deepen, with tools becoming more intuitive and responsive to user input. This symbiosis could unlock new levels of creativity and efficiency, blurring the lines between human and machine-generated content.

The democratization of AI tools promises to lower barriers to entry, enabling independent creators and small businesses to compete with larger entities. This shift could foster a more vibrant and diverse ecosystem of content and ideas, enriching the cultural landscape.

Advancements in AI ethics and governance will likely shape the trajectory of generative AI, emphasizing developing standards and frameworks that ensure responsible use. As public awareness grows, so will demands for transparency and accountability from AI developers and deploying organizations.

Finally, augmented reality (AR) and virtual reality (VR) are poised to merge with generative AI, creating immersive experiences that blur the boundaries between the digital and physical worlds. These technologies, from virtual travel to experiential learning, could change how we interact with information and each other, creating new opportunities.

In sum, generative AI's role in today's tech landscape is transformative and multifaceted. It drives innovation while raising important ethical and social questions. Its applications span industries and touch on aspects of creativity, productivity, and decision-making previously thought to be the sole domain of humans. As we navigate this evolving landscape, the promise and challenges of generative AI will undoubtedly continue to shape our world profoundly.

TWO

Unlocking the Brain of AI

Picture this: A bustling city with pathways and connections, a hub of activity where every route and decision is part of a more extensive, intricate network. This city isn't just any city; it's the bustling metropolis inside our skulls. It is a marvel of nature that has inspired one of the most groundbreaking technological advancements: neural networks. Now, let's shift our gaze from the organic to the digital, from the neurons firing in our brains to the artificial neurons that form the backbone of generative AI. In the world of digital code, we discover what enables these machines to calculate and create.

Neural Networks: The Brain Behind AI

Introduction to Neural Networks

Neural networks draw their inspiration directly from us—or, more precisely, from our brains. Just as our brains process information through a vast network of neurons, artificial neural networks (ANNs) use a web of artificial neurons to process data.

Like its biological counterpart, each artificial neuron receives input, processes it, and passes on output to the next network layer. The magic happens in the connections, or "weights," between these neurons, which are fine-tuned during training, enabling the network to learn and make increasingly accurate predictions or generate new data.

Role of Neural Networks in Generative AI

In the world of generative AI, neural networks are the star performers. They're the architects behind the scenes, meticulously crafting everything from hauntingly beautiful art pieces to eerily accurate deepfake videos. But how? It all boils down to their ability to learn patterns in the training data and use those patterns to generate new data that is similar but different. This learning and creating process is similar to that of a musician who can improvise a new piece of music that feels familiar and fresh after years of practicing scales and studying compositions.

Types of Neural Networks

Diving deeper, we find that not all neural networks are created equal. Each type has its niche and specialty, making it the perfect fit for specific tasks:

- **Convolutional neural networks (CNNs)** shine in visual data processing. They're the virtuosos behind image recognition and generation, adept at understanding the intricacies of pixels and patterns. Imagine a CNN as a keen-eyed art critic, dissecting the styles and strokes of paintings to create new masterpieces.
- **Recurrent neural networks (RNNs)** excel in handling sequential data, such as text or time series. They remember past inputs and use this memory to influence future outputs, making them ideal for tasks like language

translation or music composition. Picture an RNN as a storyteller, weaving tales where each word builds upon the last.

Challenges and Solutions

Neural networks are robust, but they have their challenges. One common problem is overfitting, where the network learns the training data too well, including all its noise and outliers, which makes it less effective with new data. Regularization techniques and dropout are strategies to prevent this, helping the network stay versatile and adaptive.

Another challenge is the sheer computational power required to train these networks, especially as they grow in size and complexity. This problem resembles an artist needing a larger studio as their canvases and projects expand. Solutions include optimizing network architectures and leveraging powerful GPUs, making it easier to scale up projects without getting bogged down by technical limitations.

In the world of neural networks, every challenge is a chance to innovate and expand the possibilities of AI. With their ability to learn, adapt, and create, these networks are not just tools but collaborators, ushering in a new era of creativity and discovery. As we stand on the brink of this new era, it's clear that the journey of generative AI, guided by the principles of neural networks, is only just beginning.

As we delve into the intricacies of neural networks, it becomes evident that they are more than mere data conduits; they are the essence of generative AI's creative prowess. From the meticulously structured layers of a CNN to the memory-laden loops of an RNN, these networks embody the fusion of technology and creativity, science and art. They remind us that at the heart of every algorithm and line of code lies a spark of inspiration, a drive to create and innovate. In this light, neural networks stand as a testament to human ingenuity and a beacon for the future of technology. AI will think, imagine, analyze, and dream in the future.

Algorithms: The Instructions AI Follows

An algorithm is at the heart of every AI marvel, from the simplest chatbot to the most complex generative AI systems. Think of an algorithm as a recipe in the grand cookbook of AI. It's a set of instructions that guides the AI in processing data, learning from it, and eventually creating something new. In the context of AI, algorithms are the maestros conducting the orchestra of data inputs, computational processes, and outputs. They are critical in dictating how an AI system behaves, learns, and evolves.

When we venture into generative AI, algorithms play a particularly fascinating role. They're not just sorting or analyzing data; they're using it to generate new creations. These algorithms are the architects of digital content, molding raw data into new forms and structures.

- **Segmentation** is the foundation of personalized marketing, enabling strategies tailored to each group's needs and preferences.
- **Generative adversarial networks (GANs)** employ two algorithms in digital tête-à-tête, generating content and evaluating its authenticity. Each iteration brings the generated output closer to indistinguishable realism.
- **Transformers** are algorithms that have revolutionized language processing. They enable machines to understand and generate human-like text based on the

context of entire sentences or pages rather than just sequential word order.

The evolution of algorithms in AI is a tale of the relentless pursuit of efficiency, accuracy, and creativity. In the early days, algorithms were simple and rigid, designed for specific tasks with clear-cut rules. However, as AI's ambitions grew, so did the complexity and sophistication of its algorithms. From bare decision trees to deep learning and beyond, each leap forward in algorithmic design has unlocked new possibilities for AI. The development of neural networks and later deep learning marked significant milestones, enabling machines to learn from vast amounts of data and generate complex and nuanced outputs.

The impact of an algorithm on the quality and realism of AI output is profound. The choice of algorithm can mean the difference between a generative AI that creates stunningly realistic images and one that produces mere abstractions. It's like the difference between a beginner painter and a master artist. At the same time, both can create a portrait. Their work's depth, detail, and lifelikeness will vary significantly based on their skills and techniques.

In generative AI, the quality of output hinges on the algorithm's ability to learn from and interpret the training data effectively. Algorithms that can capture the subtleties and complexities of the data will generate more realistic, diverse, and creative outputs. For instance, an algorithm trained on a dataset of classical paintings will learn to create new artworks that echo the styles and techniques of the old masters. In contrast, one trained in contemporary music can compose new songs that resonate with modern sensibilities.

Moreover, the evolution of algorithms has led to the development of models that can generate content across multiple domains, from visual arts to literature and everything in between. These cross-domain algorithms are the frontier of generative AI, offering a glimpse into a future where AI can seamlessly blend ideas and inspirations from various sources to create entirely new forms of expression.

In this light, algorithms are more than just the backbone of AI; they are the creative force behind it. They shape how AI interacts with the world, learns from it, and contributes to it, making them central to the ongoing evolution of generative AI. As we continue to push the boundaries of what AI can achieve, algorithms will only grow in importance, guiding AI systems as they explore new frontiers of creativity and innovation.

Data: The Fuel of Generative AI

Even the most advanced car will only move with the right fuel. In the same way, generative AI needs data to power its creativity. This data isn't just numbers and facts; it allows the algorithms to learn, adapt, and create. The quality, diversity, and amount of data directly affect what AI can do. The output depends on the quality of the input.

We're not simply dumping data into a digital hopper when we talk about feeding AI. The process is more nuanced, involving careful selection, preparation, and refinement of data to ensure it's ready for consumption. This process can be broken down into several key stages:

- **Gathering**: Data collection is the first step, where raw data is sourced from various channels. This might involve scraping images from the web for a visual AI project,

compiling text from books and articles for a language model, or collecting sensor data for predictive modeling in industrial applications.
- **Cleaning**: Raw data often comes with noise—irrelevant information, errors, or inconsistencies. Just like you wash fruits before eating, data must be cleaned to ensure the AI isn't learning from bad information.
- **Labeling**: Data needs labels for supervised learning models. These labels help the AI understand and learn from different examples, similar to how organizing your music collection by genre makes it easier to find and understand.
- **Augmentation**: Sometimes, more than the available data is needed. Data augmentation techniques, like flipping images or altering text, can expand a dataset, giving the AI more angles to learn from without needing entirely new data.

Despite meticulous collection and processing, data for generative AI is fraught with challenges:

- **Bias**: If the data collected is biased or not representative, the AI's output will also be biased. It's like learning to cook from a cookbook with only pasta recipes; the AI will have a limited perspective on what's possible.
- **Privacy**: Collecting personal data raises significant privacy concerns. Using someone's photos or messages without consent to train AI models can lead to ethical and legal issues.
- **Quality**: Poor data can derail an AI project before it begins. Imagine learning French from a textbook with typos and grammatical errors; the learning process would be confusing, if not downright misleading.

Facing these challenges head-on, the AI community has devised innovative solutions to ensure generative AI has the high-quality fuel it needs:

- **Synthetic Data Generation**: When enough real-world data or privacy issues prevent its use, synthetic data steps in. Algorithms generate this data to mimic real data without privacy issues. It provides new material for AI to learn from, even when data isn't available.
- **Federated Learning**: This technique allows AI models to learn from data stored on individual devices without transferring it. A teacher could help students improve their essays without ever reading them, protecting their privacy while offering guidance.
- **Differential Privacy**: By adding "noise" to the data or its analysis, differential privacy allows AI to learn patterns without accessing or revealing individual data points. This way, the AI understands the general idea without exposing specific details.
- **Bias Detection Tools**: AI researchers have developed tools to detect and correct biases in datasets. These tools scrutinize data through various lenses, identifying and mitigating skewness or underrepresentation before they can influence the AI's learning process.

In the world of generative AI, data is both the foundation and the frontier. It's the raw material for new digital creations, the inspiration for AI's outputs, and the measure of its intelligence. The journey from raw data to a generative masterpiece is complex and challenging, but AI developers and researchers navigate it daily with innovative tools and techniques. Data remains central as we keep exploring and expanding generative AI, highlighting the technology's potential and our responsibility in using it.

Machine Learning vs. Deep Learning in Generative AI

In the AI landscape, where creativity and computation intertwine, two significant methodologies emerge: machine learning and deep learning. Both are the engine room for the dazzling array of generative AI applications we see today. Yet, they operate under different paradigms with unique strengths and specializations.

Machine learning is the science of getting computers to act without being explicitly programmed. It's about teaching machines to learn from data, identify patterns, and make decisions. Deep learning, a subset of machine learning, takes this a notch higher. It draws inspiration from the human brain's architecture to develop algorithms called neural networks capable of learning in-depth patterns in large data sets.

Machine learning is like a young child learning and recognizing new objects by features and direct instruction, while deep learning is like a teenager understanding complex concepts, inferring from context, and grasping nuances due to advanced cognitive processing.

Deep Learning's Advantage

Deep learning shines in generative AI for its proficiency in handling and generating complex data patterns. Its neural networks, composed of multiple layers, allow for an intricate understanding and manipulation of data. This depth enables the creation of highly detailed and nuanced outputs, whether they be images that rival photographs in realism or prose indistinguishable from that written by human hands.

The advantage of deep learning comes from its ability to process data hierarchically. Initial layers might recognize an image's simple patterns or features, like edges. Subsequent layers combine these elements to identify more complex structures, such as shapes or objects, and higher layers still synthesize this information to understand entire scenes or concepts. This layered learning approach mirrors the depth and complexity of human creativity, making deep learning particularly suited to generative tasks.

Applications in Generative AI

Both machine learning and deep learning find their applications in generative AI, each bringing its strengths to the fore:

- Machine learning algorithms have been adept at tasks like generating simple texts or music based on pattern recognition. For example, they can analyze a corpus of classical music, learn the patterns, and produce new compositions that reflect learned styles.
- Deep learning takes this further, enabling more complex and creative applications. Generative adversarial networks (GANs), powered by deep learning, have created realistic images and artworks from scratch. These models have also been instrumental in developing sophisticated natural language processing tools that can write coherent and contextually rich texts, dialogues, or even poetry.

The range of applications for these technologies in generative AI is broad and continually expanding. The innovation potential is boundless, from designing virtual environments that adapt dynamically to user interactions to creating fashion designs that predict and set trends. In healthcare, deep learning models generate synthetic medical images for research, enhancing studies while preserving patient privacy. Meanwhile, machine learning algorithms in video games create levels or content that adapt to a player's style, keeping games challenging and engaging.

Future Directions

The horizon for machine learning and deep learning in generative AI is vast and filled with potential. We stand on the brink of a future where these technologies will enhance human creativity and open new avenues for exploration and expression. Some future directions include:

- **Cross-Disciplinary Innovation**: As these technologies mature, their application across various fields will lead to groundbreaking cross-disciplinary innovations. For instance, combining generative AI with biotechnology could create new materials inspired by nature but designed digitally.
- **Augmented Creativity**: Tools that enhance human creativity through collaboration with AI will become more sophisticated. Artists, designers, and creators will collaborate with AI, using it as a partner to explore new creative possibilities.
- **Personalization and Customization**: In the consumer space, machine learning and deep learning will drive the next level of personalization, creating products, services, and experiences uniquely tailored to individual preferences and needs.
- **Ethical and Responsible AI**: As generative AI becomes more powerful, ensuring its ethical use will be paramount. This will involve developing frameworks and guidelines that govern the creation and use of AI-generated content, focusing on transparency, fairness, and accountability.

As we navigate this exciting future, the distinction between machine learning and deep learning in generative AI will become less about their differences and more about how they can complement each other. Together, they form a powerful toolkit for innovation that promises to redefine the boundaries of creativity and technology. The journey ahead for generative AI is not just about harnessing these technologies but about exploring the endless possibilities they unlock for human expression and invention.

Key Technologies Powering Generative AI

Exploring the dynamic world of generative AI reveals that this isn't a solo act. Behind the curtain lies a symphony of technologies, each playing its part in orchestrating the creations that seem to blur the lines between human-made and machine-generated. From the robust hardware that forms the backbone of AI's computational might to the sophisticated software frameworks that serve as the creative palette for AI developers, the ensemble is as complex as it is fascinating.

Overview of Technologies

At the core of generative AI's capabilities are two fundamental elements: hardware and software. On the one hand, we have advancements in hardware, such as GPUs and specialized AI processors, which provide the computational horsepower necessary for training large and complex AI models. On the other hand, software frameworks and tools, like TensorFlow and PyTorch, offer the environment and building blocks for designing, training, and deploying these models. Together, they create a fertile ground for generative AI to flourish, pushing the boundaries of what machines can make.

Computational Power

Generative AI's appetite for computational power is insatiable. Training models that mimic or surpass human creativity require immense processing capabilities. Initially designed for rendering graphics, GPUs have emerged as the workhorses of AI computation, capable of performing parallel operations essential for the heavy lifting in training AI models. TPUs and other AI-dedicated hardware further streamline these processes, offering optimizations that significantly reduce training times and energy consumption. This surge in computational resources has democratized access to generative AI, enabling a more comprehensive array of creators and innovators to experiment and build with these technologies.

Software Frameworks and Tools

The brilliance of generative AI lies in its hardware and the sophistication of its software. TensorFlow and PyTorch stand out as the leading lights in this domain, offering flexible, powerful, and intuitive platforms for AI development. These frameworks provide the libraries and tools necessary for crafting neural networks, designing algorithms, and processing data within environments that support rapid iteration and experimentation. Their widespread adoption has fostered a vibrant community of developers and researchers, further accelerating advancements in generative AI.

- **TensorFlow**, developed by Google, excels in its scalability and deployment capabilities, making it ideal for projects transitioning from research to production environments.
- **PyTorch**, backed by Facebook, shines with its dynamic computation graph and user-friendly interface, offering a preferred choice for researchers and those delving into AI for the first time.

Together, these frameworks serve as the canvases on which the future of generative AI is painted, encapsulating the complexities of AI development into tools that empower creators to bring their visions to life.

Emerging Technologies

As we peer into the horizon, several emerging technologies promise further to elevate the capabilities and accessibility of generative AI. Quantum computing, with its potential to process information at unprecedented speeds, could dramatically reduce the time required for training AI models, making more complex and creative algorithms feasible. Edge computing brings AI processing closer to where data is generated, enabling real-time generative applications in environments where latency is critical. Meanwhile, advancements in AI chips and neural network architectures continue to refine the efficiency and effectiveness of generative models, ensuring that AI's future is more powerful, sustainable, and accessible.

Each of these technologies plays a crucial role in the evolving landscape of generative AI, offering new pathways for exploration and innovation. As we navigate this landscape, the interplay between hardware and software, computational might, and creative algorithms remains at the heart of generative AI's journey. It's a journey that redefines the limits of machine creativity and offers a mirror to our innovative processes, challenging us to reimagine the relationship between humans and machines.

In this chapter, we've lifted the veil on the technologies that fuel generative AI, revealing a world where creativity is not bounded by human limitations but enhanced by machine capabilities. From the robust computational power that drives AI models to the sophisticated software frameworks that nurture their development, the foundation for generative AI is as solid as it is dynamic. Emerging technologies promise to push these boundaries even further, opening up new horizons for what machines can create and how we interact with their creations.

As we turn the page, the narrative of generative AI continues to unfold, a testament to human ingenuity and the endless potential of technology to augment our creative spirit. The journey ahead is as exciting as it is uncertain—a voyage into the unknown where the only limit is our imagination. As we venture forth, the tools and technologies we've explored in this chapter will light the way, guiding us toward a future where AI not only complements but elevates human creativity to new heights.

THREE

Tailoring Your World with Generative AI

Imagine flipping through a photo album—each picture tells a unique story, and each moment captured is a personalized memory. Now, think of generative AI as a kind of digital photo album. Still, instead of memories, it's crafting experiences, content, and interactions that are uniquely tailored to you. It's about turning the everyday into something that's not just generic but genuinely yours. From the shows you binge-watch to the games you lose yourself in, generative AI quietly reshapes our digital landscapes into personalized playgrounds.

Tailored Content Creation

Thanks to generative AI, platforms like Netflix or Spotify have become more than just content libraries; they're like personal entertainment concierges. Here's how it unfolds:

- **Netflix** analyzes your watch history, ratings you've given, and even what you've searched for to recommend shows and movies. It's not just about the genres you like; it's about understanding the nuances—maybe you have a

thing for strong female leads or a penchant for Nordic noir. Generative AI digs into these patterns, creating a hand-picked viewing experience.
- **Spotify** works its magic similarly with music. It's not just throwing random playlists at you; it's creating a soundtrack for your life. Each song you skip, save, or play on repeat teaches Spotify's AI about your tastes. Over time, it stitches together playlists that might introduce you to a new favorite band or remind you of an old gem you'd forgotten. It's like having a friend who knows your music taste perfectly and makes you mixtapes.

Dynamic News Feeds

Scroll through your social media, and you'll notice how your feed knows your interests. That's generative AI at work again, curating your news feed:

- It starts with your interactions—the posts you like, share, or comment on. Generative AI mixes this data with information about the accounts you follow and even factors in how much time you spend on different posts.
- The result? A feed that prioritizes content you're likely to engage with, ensuring that what's relevant to you is aware of the noise. It's about making your social media experience more meaningful and less about mindless scrolling.

Interactive Gaming Environments

Video games have evolved from linear narratives to worlds that adapt and respond to the player. Generative AI is a big part of this shift:

- Picture a game where the environment changes based on your decisions, where side quests and characters react dynamically to your actions. This isn't just about creating a replayable match; it's about making each playthrough uniquely yours.
- Developers use generative AI to create these adaptive environments. This could alter storylines, generate new challenges, or craft evolving worlds. The game "listens" and "learns" from how you play, tailoring the experience just for you.

Customized Learning Materials

Education is getting a personal touch with generative AI, moving away from one-size-fits-all to something that adapts to individual learning styles and needs:

- Imagine a learning platform that adjusts the difficulty level of problems in real time, offers additional resources when you're struggling, or skips ahead when you're breezing through the material. That's generative AI in action.
- It's not just about making learning more efficient; it's about making it more engaging. By tailoring content to fit each learner's pace and style, education becomes a more inclusive and practical experience.

In these examples, generative AI isn't just changing how we consume content or interact with digital environments; it's redefining personalization. It's about crafting experiences that feel as unique to you as your fingerprint, ensuring that your digital world reflects your preferences and behaviors and is an extension of them. As we navigate these increasingly personalized landscapes, it's clear that generative AI is not just tailoring our digital experiences; it's reshaping our expectations of the digital world, setting a new standard for personalization that's as dynamic and unique as we are.

Smart Homes and AI: A Practical Utopia

In a world where time is as precious as ever, our homes are becoming more than just places to rest; they're evolving into intelligent environments that anticipate our needs and simplify our lives. Generative AI is at the forefront of this transformation, making smart homes not just a concept but a living, breathing reality.

Automating Home Tasks

The magic starts with the mundane—managing daily chores and household tasks. Imagine your home knows when to start the dishwasher for maximum energy efficiency or can predict the best time to do the laundry based on your schedule and energy rates. This isn't just convenient; it's eco-friendly and cost-effective. Here's how generative AI fits into home automation:

- **Learning Routines**: Your smart home observes and learns from your routines, understanding when you will likely need specific tasks.
- **Predictive Scheduling**: Using this knowledge, you can schedule tasks like vacuuming or lawn mowing at times that cause the least disruption to your day.
- **Energy Management**: Generative AI analyzes energy consumption patterns to optimize appliance use, reduce waste and save on bills.

Enhanced Security Systems

Safety is a key part of the smart home concept, and generative AI is taking home security systems to a new level. Beyond traditional alarms and surveillance, AI-powered security systems can differentiate between routine and unusual activities, alerting you only when there's a genuine cause for concern. This level of precision means:

- **Adaptive Alerts**: You're immediately notified if an unfamiliar face is at the door or if there's an unusual movement pattern at odd hours.
- **Voice Recognition**: Advanced systems can even recognize distress signals or unusual sounds, offering protection.
- **Continuous Learning**: The more the system observes, the better it distinguishes between benign and suspicious activities, reducing false alarms and enhancing peace of mind.

Personalized Home Assistants

Voice-activated assistants have become the friendly voices that fill our homes, offering more than just weather updates or playing our favorite tunes. Powered by generative AI, these assistants are evolving into personal aides who know us better than we know ourselves. They're not just responding to our commands but anticipating our needs, whether reminding us of upcoming appointments or suggesting a dinner recipe based on what's in the fridge. This leap in personalization means:

- **Contextual Interactions**: Conversations with your AI assistant feel natural and fluid, with the assistant understanding the words, their context, and intent.

- **Proactive Assistance**: Instead of waiting for instructions, your assistant might suggest the perfect playlist for your evening workout or remind you to call a friend on their birthday.
- **Seamless Integration**: These assistants become the central hub of your smart home, controlling devices and systems with an understanding of your preferences and habits.

Future Prospects

Peering into the future, the possibilities for smart homes powered by generative AI are as vast as the imagination allows. Here are a few glimpses into what might be on the horizon:

- **Emotional Intelligence**: Future smart homes might understand our habits and moods and adjust lighting, music, and even scents to improve our well-being.
- **Predictive Health Monitoring**: Imagine a home that monitors your health, predicting potential issues before they become severe and coordinating with healthcare providers as needed.
- **Fully Autonomous Homes**: We might see homes that manage themselves entirely, from ordering groceries and maintenance to adjusting environments for optimal comfort and efficiency.

In this evolving landscape, generative AI doesn't just automate tasks or enhance security; it crafts environments that adapt to and anticipate our needs, making our homes true sanctuaries in the digital age. As these technologies advance, our homes will become more in tune with our lives, offering comfort, convenience, and a touch of magic in our daily routines.

Enhancing Creativity in Art and Music

Artists and musicians find themselves at a crossroads of tradition and innovation in a world where the brush meets the pixel and melodies intertwine with codes. Generative AI, a tool once thought to belong solely to tech enthusiasts, is now a companion to creativity, urging the curious and the bold to rethink the boundaries of what's possible in art and music.

AI in Art Creation

The canvas is no longer just a physical entity awaiting the touch of paint. Still, it has expanded into the digital, where algorithms generate vistas limited only by imagination. Artists engage with generative AI to push the envelope, creating artworks that challenge our perceptions of creativity and authorship. Here's how:

- **Collaboration with the Machine**: Artists feed sketches, concepts, or even moods into AI systems, churning out interpretations or expansions of these inputs. This process can result in a single piece or a series, each reflecting a blend of human intention and machine interpretation.
- **Exploration of New Styles**: By analyzing vast datasets of historical art, AI can mimic styles from Baroque to Bauhaus, offering artists a palette far broader than traditional methods could allow. Some artists use this capability to fuse styles, creating pieces that blend impressionism's fluidity with modernism's stark lines.
- **Infinite Iterations**: With generative AI, artists can explore variations on a theme at an unimaginable scale. Inputting a basic design can yield countless renditions,

each tweaking colors, forms, or textures, providing a rich array of choices for further development.

Music Composition

The symphony hall, too, is buzzing with the possibilities AI brings. Composers and musicians employ AI to compose music that resonates, surprises, and delights, often in ways human minds might not conceive. This includes:

- **Algorithmic Compositions**: AI analyzes vast music collections to understand patterns, structures, and elements that define different genres. Musicians can then direct the AI to create compositions in a chosen style or blend styles, crafting familiar yet fresh pieces.
- **Dynamic Soundscapes**: For immersive environments, such as games or virtual reality experiences, AI generates adaptive soundscapes that respond to user interactions. This dynamic composition process creates an audio experience that's as alive and responsive as the visual elements.
- **Collaborative Performance**: AI isn't just for the studio; it's also taking the stage. Projects are emerging where live musicians perform alongside AI, responding to and interacting with music generated in real time. This collaboration between humans and machines opens new avenues for improvisation and performance.

Collaborative Art Projects

The intersection of AI and creativity is fertile ground for collaboration between artists, machines, and communities. Projects around the globe showcase how collective human creativity combined with AI can result in stunning, thought-provoking works:

- **Global Art Exchanges**: Online platforms enable artists to submit works for AI to remix, reinterpret, or integrate into larger collaborative pieces. These projects highlight the diversity of human creativity while showcasing the unifying potential of technology.
- **Interactive Installations**: Some exhibitions invite participants to contribute inputs—text, drawings, or movement—that AI translates into real-time art. These installations break down the barriers between creator and audience, offering immersive experiences that evolve with each interaction.

Ethical Considerations

As generative AI entwines more deeply with creative endeavors, it brings to light questions that echo through the galleries and concert halls. The dialogue around ethics, authorship, and the essence of creativity grows louder and more nuanced:

- **Who Is the Creator**: Who claims creativity when AI generates art or music based on human input? This question challenges traditional notions of authorship and urges reevaluating how we attribute and value creative work.
- **Preservation of Originality**: There's a delicate balance between drawing inspiration from existing works and infringing upon them. AI's ability to analyze and replicate styles raises concerns about preserving originality and the potential for unintentional imitation.

- **Access and Bias**: The datasets used to train AI can carry biases, reflecting historical inequalities in the art and music worlds. Ensuring these tools are accessible to diverse creators is crucial to preventing the perpetuation of these biases in future works.

In navigating these ethical waters, the creative community, technologists, and policymakers engage in conversations that will shape the future of art and music in the AI era. The discourse ensures that, as we move forward, we do so with a keen awareness of the implications, fostering an environment where creativity flourishes in harmony with technology.

As generative AI becomes more integrated into creativity, artists and musicians are entering an exciting new era. It's a time full of potential, where digital and traditional methods combine to create new forms of human expression. In this ever-changing landscape, the only sure thing is that things will keep evolving, offering endless possibilities for innovation and brilliance.

Generative AI in Personal Health and Fitness

In health and fitness, the personal touch makes all the difference. Imagine a world where your workout routine and diet plan are as unique as your DNA, where mental health support is always at your fingertips, tailored just for you. This isn't a distant dream—it's the reality being shaped by generative AI, making strides toward a future where personal health and fitness are not just about general guidelines but bespoke solutions.

Customized Fitness Programs

Fitness is not one-size-fits-all. What works wonders for one might not work for another. Recognizing this, generative AI designs fitness programs as individual as fingerprints. It starts with your health data—everything from your age, weight, and height to more nuanced information like genetic predispositions and current fitness levels. Here's how it unfolds:

- **Data Analysis**: Generative AI sifts through this data, spotting patterns and drawing insights.
- **Goal Setting**: Whether you want to lose weight, gain muscle, or enhance endurance, AI tailors the program to your goals.
- **Dynamic Adjustments**: As you progress, the AI tweaks your program based on feedback from your performance, ensuring you're always on the most effective path toward your goals.

This process ensures that your fitness journey is not just about following a set routine but also about evolving and adapting as you do.

Mental Health Applications

In a world increasingly acknowledging mental health's importance, generative AI offers a beacon of hope. It's powering tools that provide support and guidance, making mental health care more accessible. Therapy chatbots aren't just pre-programmed responders; they are AI systems that learn from each interaction to offer more personalized support. Here's what they can do:

- **Immediate Support**: They're available round the clock, offering a listening ear when needed.
- **Personalized Conversations**: These chatbots tailor their guidance to fit your emotional and psychological needs by learning from your responses over time.

- **Resource Provision**: Besides conversation, they can recommend specific exercises, readings, or even professional services based on your unique situation.

These tools don't replace human therapists but offer a valuable support layer, bridging gaps in the mental health care system.

Wearable Technology

The rise of wearable tech has been a game-changer in personal health monitoring. With generative AI, these devices are becoming even more intelligent. They're not just tracking your steps or heart rate but interpreting this data to offer insights and recommendations tailored just for you. Here's a glimpse into how generative AI elevates wearable technology:

- **Health Insights**: AI can identify health trends and potential concerns by analyzing activity levels, sleep patterns, and vital signs.
- **Personalized Recommendations**: From suggesting more rest on a day when your sleep quality was low to recommending hydration levels based on your activity, the advice is always personalized.
- **Motivation and Goals**: AI helps set achievable health goals based on your data, keeping you motivated with personalized challenges and milestones.

This synergy between wearable tech and generative AI turns data into actionable insights, making health monitoring more intuitive and effective.

Future of Personalized Medicine

The true potential of generative AI in health and fitness lies in its promise to revolutionize personalized medicine. The future it's paving the way toward is one where treatment plans and medication management are not based on broad demographic categories but on each individual's unique genetic makeup and lifestyle. Here's what's on the horizon:

- **Bespoke Treatment Plans**: AI can analyze genetic data, medical history, and current health status to formulate treatment plans uniquely suited to each patient's needs.
- **Medication Management**: By understanding how different bodies react to medications, AI can predict and manage side effects, ensuring patients receive the most effective dosages with minimal risks.
- **Predictive Health**: Beyond treating existing conditions, generative AI can predict potential health issues before they arise, offering a window for preventive measures specifically tailored to reduce individual risk.

This vision of personalized medicine promises more effective treatments and a proactive approach to health, where prevention is just as tailored as the cure.

In weaving through the domains of fitness programs, mental health support, wearable technology, and the promising horizon of personalized medicine, it's clear that generative AI is not just transforming how we approach health and fitness—it's redefining it. Turning data into customized insights and actions is placing each of us at the center of our health journey, making wellness not just a goal but a profoundly personal journey.

AI-Enhanced Educational Tools

In education, the one-size-fits-all approach is becoming a relic of the past. It's about time, too. With the dynamism and diversity of learners' needs, abilities, and aspirations, education demands a more personalized touch. Generative AI is the architect of this new era, crafting learning experiences that adapt to and grow with each student. It's not just teaching; it's nurturing a love for learning.

Adaptive Learning Platforms

Imagine a classroom where every student receives instruction explicitly tailored to their pace, style, and level of understanding. This is no longer wishful thinking but a reality made possible by adaptive learning platforms powered by generative AI. These platforms are game-changers, offering a myriad of benefits:

- **Individualized Pacing**: Students no longer have to feel rushed through topics they find challenging or held back by lessons they already understand. AI adjusts the pace based on real-time performance and feedback.
- **Focused Attention**: Areas needing improvement receive more attention. For example, if a student struggles with fractions, the AI generates more exercises targeting this concept, complete with explanations and examples.
- **Engagement and Motivation**: Students are more engaged and motivated by content that aligns with their interests and learning goals. It's learning designed around what they need to know and what they love to discover.

Interactive Simulations

For subjects that traditionally challenge students, like complex scientific concepts or advanced mathematics, generative AI brings fresh air. Through interactive simulations, learners can visualize and manipulate variables in real time, observing outcomes and gaining insights that were once confined to textbook margins. These simulations:

- **Bring Abstract Concepts to Life**: The water cycle, planetary movements, or chemical reactions transform from static diagrams into dynamic, interactive experiences.
- **Encourage Experimentation**: Students can test hypotheses, change parameters, and see the effects immediately, fostering a hands-on approach to learning.
- **Cater to Different Learning Styles**: Whether a student learns best by seeing, doing, or hearing, interactive simulations offer a multi-sensory learning environment that enhances comprehension and retention.

Language Learning

The journey to fluency in a new language is fraught with challenges. Still, AI-driven language learning apps are smoothing the path. These apps personalize the learning experience, adjusting to the user's proficiency level and preferred learning style. They offer:

- **Customized Lessons**: From beginner to advanced, each lesson is tailored to challenge the learner appropriately, ensuring steady progress without overwhelming them.
- **Real-World Context**: Generative AI incorporates current events, popular culture, and user interests into language lessons, making learning relevant and engaging.
- **Interactive Practice**: Conversations with AI tutors provide immediate feedback and corrections, simulating real-life interactions and boosting conversational skills.

Challenges and Opportunities

While integrating AI into education opens new horizons, it has hurdles. Ensuring equitable access to technology, safeguarding student data, and maintaining the human touch in teaching are just a few of the challenges ahead. Yet, these challenges are not roadblocks but stepping stones, leading us to a future where education is more inclusive, practical, and inspiring. The opportunities are limitless:

- **Bridging the Gap**: AI can help level the playing field by offering high-quality, personalized learning experiences to students in remote or underserved areas.
- **Lifelong Learning**: With AI, education extends beyond the classroom, supporting learners of all ages in pursuing knowledge and skills.
- **Teacher Empowerment**: Rather than replacing teachers, AI is a powerful tool in their arsenal, freeing up time for them to focus on what they do best—inspiring and guiding students.

As we wrap up our exploration of generative AI's role in revolutionizing education, it's clear this technology is not just changing how we learn but reshaping our very approach to knowledge and skill acquisition. It's a journey from passive absorption to active exploration, from standardized teaching to personalized learning experiences that ignite curiosity and foster a lifelong love for learning. With generative AI, we're not just looking at the future of education; we're stepping into it, ready to embrace the boundless opportunities it brings.

As we turn our gaze from the classrooms and screens to the broader canvas of society, the impact of generative AI extends far beyond individual learning. It's shaping a world where technology and humanity converge, promising a future prosperous with possibility and innovation.

FOUR

The New Frontiers of Customer Experience

Picture a bustling marketplace—not the ancient kind with stalls and shouts, but its modern digital counterpart. It's vast, it's vibrant, and it's personalized down to the last pixel. In this space, every interaction feels less like a transaction and more like a conversation with a good friend who knows your tastes and preferences. This isn't a far-off dream; it's today's customer experience, redefined by generative AI.

In this chapter, we peel back the layers of how businesses use AI to transform how we shop, engage, and find satisfaction in the digital age. From chatbots that know what you're looking for to designing interfaces that adapt to your needs, AI isn't just changing the game; it's creating a whole new playing field.

AI-Powered Chatbots

Imagine walking into a store and being greeted by a salesperson who knows precisely what you need, even if you're unsure. That's the power of AI-powered chatbots. They're the digital equivalent of that intuitive salesperson, always on hand to guide you through your shopping journey. Here's the scoop:

- **Instant Support**: These chatbots are there 24/7, ready to answer questions, track down products, or troubleshoot issues. It's like having a personal shopper in your pocket, always ready to help.
- **Learning Your Preferences**: The more you interact, the wiser they get. Whether you're into vintage vinyl or the latest tech gadgets, these chatbots tailor their suggestions to fit your unique taste.
- **Seamless Shopping**: They can handle everything from finding the right size to checking out, making the whole process as smooth as silk.

User Experience Design

Think about the last time you used an app or website and how everything flowed. That's generative AI at work in user experience (UX) design. It's about creating digital spaces that aren't just easy to navigate but anticipate what you want. Here's what's happening behind the scenes:

- **Smart Layouts**: Websites and apps adjust in real-time, presenting information and options based on what you'll most likely need next. It's like they're reading your mind.
- **Accessibility**: AI ensures everyone gets the same high-quality experience, adapting interfaces for those with disabilities and making the digital world more inclusive.
- **Engagement**: Interactive elements keep users engaged, turning browsing into an enjoyable and efficient experience.

Customer Insights

Behind every click, there's a wealth of information, and generative AI is the key to unlocking it. Businesses are using AI to dive deep into customer data, uncovering insights that can drive innovation and improve services. Here's the lowdown:

- **Trend Spotting**: AI sifts through data at lightning speed, identifying patterns that can signal the next big thing. It's like having a crystal ball for market trends.
- **Feedback Analysis**: Every review, comment, or social media post is a goldmine of feedback. AI analyzes this information, helping businesses understand what's working and what's not.
- **Customization**: With these insights, businesses can customize their offerings, ensuring they always hit the mark.

Personalization in Retail

We've all felt the thrill of finding something that seems like it was made just for us. AI is making that moment happen more often. In online and in-store retail, generative AI unprecedentedly personalizes the shopping experience. Here's how:

- **Product Recommendations**: AI curates a selection of products you'll likely love based on your shopping history and preferences. It's like your own personal catalog.
- **Dynamic Pricing**: Have you ever noticed how prices can change depending on when you shop? AI adjusts pricing in real time, offering deals that are hard to resist.
- **In-Store Experience**: For those who prefer brick-and-mortar stores, AI enhances the experience with virtual

fitting rooms and intelligent mirrors that suggest items based on your trying.

In this chapter, we've just scratched the surface of how generative AI is revolutionizing the customer experience. From the moment you start browsing to the after-sales support, AI is there, making every step of the journey smoother, more enjoyable, and deeply personal. It's not just about selling products; it's about building relationships, understanding needs, and creating value beyond the transaction. In the bustling digital marketplace of today, AI is the secret sauce that's turning shopping from a chore into an adventure.

Streamlining Operations and Manufacturing

In the bustling world of production and distribution, where every second counts and efficiency is king, generative AI is stepping up as the silent powerhouse driving transformation. It's redefining what it means to operate at the cutting edge, making the complex dance of manufacturing and logistics look almost effortless. Let's peel back the curtain on this dynamic shift, exploring how AI is reshaping the backbone of our global economy.

Supply Chain Optimization

Navigating the intricate web of supply chains is no small feat. It's a delicate balance, where a single hiccup can ripple through the system, causing delays and disruptions far down the line. This is where AI acts as the ultimate conductor, ensuring every part of the supply chain moves in perfect harmony. It's about predictive analytics—AI models digest mountains of data, from weather patterns affecting shipping routes to factory output rates, identifying potential bottlenecks before they become blockades. The result? Recommendations for routing, inventory management, and even supplier selection are optimized for efficiency, keeping the wheels of commerce turning smoothly.

- **Real-Time Adjustments**: AI doesn't just predict; it adapts. As conditions change, it recalibrates, suggesting immediate changes to keep things flowing.
- **Visibility and Transparency**: With AI, every stakeholder gains a bird's-eye view of the supply chain, fostering trust and collaboration.

Manufacturing Automation

Stepping onto the factory floor, the impact of AI is unmistakable. Robots and machines work in sync, with each movement precise and purposeful. But it's the intelligence behind the automation that's truly revolutionary. AI oversees production lines, orchestrating every detail, from the speed of conveyor belts to the timing of robotic arms. Tasks that once required human hands are now entrusted to AI for speed, accuracy, and consistency. Quality control, once a thorough process of manual checks, is now the domain of AI, capable of spotting minor imperfections faster than the human eye.

- **Adaptive Production Lines**: AI can adjust manufacturing processes on the fly, easily accommodating custom orders or design changes.
- **Enhanced Safety**: AI minimizes workplace hazards by taking over high-risk tasks, keeping human workers safe from harm.

Predictive Maintenance

The heartbeat of any operation is its machinery, and a single failure can bring everything to a standstill. Predictive maintenance, powered by generative AI, changes the game. It's about listening to the whispers of wear and tear, using sensor data to predict when a machine might falter. This foresight allows maintenance to be scheduled at just the right time, preventing breakdowns without unnecessary downtime.

- **Cost Reduction**: Avoiding significant repairs and downtime slashes costs significantly, making operations more financially predictable.
- **Extended Equipment Lifespan**: Regular, data-driven maintenance extends the life of machinery, maximizing the return on investment.

Logistics and Distribution

Finally, let's zoom out to the grand stage of logistics and distribution. In this arena, AI is the mastermind of optimizing routes in real time, ensuring that products move from factory to consumer with unmatched efficiency. It's a complex puzzle with countless variables, from traffic conditions to delivery windows. Generative AI takes it all in stride, calculating the most efficient paths, reducing fuel consumption, and ensuring timely deliveries.

- **Dynamic Routing**: There are no longer static routes; AI adjusts paths based on real-time traffic data, weather conditions, and customer availability.
- **Eco-Friendly Operations**: AI contributes to greener operations by optimizing routes and loads, reducing deliveries' carbon footprint.

In each of these facets—from the supply chain to the factory floor, from maintenance schedules to the open roads of logistics—generative AI is not just a tool but a transformative force. It's enabling precision, efficiency, and adaptability that sets a new standard for what's possible in operations and manufacturing. This quiet revolution is streamlining the backbone of our economy, ensuring that products reach us faster, safer, and more sustainably than ever before.

AI in Marketing: Personalization at Scale

In the bustling marketing world, where messages fly faster than the speed of thought and consumers are bombarded from all sides, standing out is the game's name. This is where the magic of AI steps in, turning the vast ocean of data into a tailored stream that reaches the right person at the right time with the right message. The era of casting wide nets is over; precision fishing is in, and AI is the savvy fisherman leading the charge.

Targeted Advertising

Gone are the days of billboard ads meant for everyone, yet no one in particular. AI has flipped the script, making advertising a personal affair. It's all about digging into the digital footprints left by users across the web. Each click, search, and purchase tells a story, and AI is the keen listener piecing it together. The outcome is a mosaic of user behavior and preferences, which AI uses to craft advertising campaigns that hit home.

- For instance, AI notes if someone's been eyeing hiking gear online. The next thing they know, ads for the latest trail shoes or eco-friendly water bottles appear in their feed.
- But it's not just about following cues. AI predicts future needs based on past behavior. For example, someone who bought a new camera might start seeing ads for photography classes or picture-perfect travel experiences.

This targeted approach transforms advertising from an intrusion to a welcome suggestion, making the whole experience more engaging and less invasive.

Content Generation

In content-heavy marketing, keeping your audience engaged can be challenging. This is where AI lends a hand, or rather, a pen. Creating content, from snappy social media posts to insightful email campaigns, is no longer a human endeavor. With its language processing capabilities, AI is now a co-author, generating relevant and resonant content.

- Picture an email campaign that feels like it's been written just for you, touching on topics you care about. That's AI, using insights from your interactions to tailor content.
- Or think of social media posts that reflect the latest trends and conversations happening in real time. Again, that's AI keeping its finger on the pulse and ensuring the brand stays relevant and relatable.

This collaboration between human creativity and AI efficiency means that brands can stay on top of their content game, keeping their audience engaged and interested.

Customer Segmentation

Understanding your audience is one thing; breaking it into actionable segments is another. AI excels at precisely slicing through data to group customers based on various factors, from demographics to behavior. This segmentation is the cornerstone of personalized marketing, allowing for strategies that cater to each group's specific needs and preferences.

- Imagine identifying not just the broad strokes of your audience but the intricate patterns within. Millennials who love adventure sports, parents looking for educational toys, and tech enthusiasts eager for the next big thing—AI identifies these segments, making it possible to tailor marketing efforts to each group.
- It predicts how different segments might respond to new products or campaigns, allowing businesses to fine-tune their strategies for maximum impact.

This deep dive into customer segmentation means marketing efforts can be more focused, effective, and, ultimately, more successful.

ROI Analysis

Understanding what works and what doesn't is crucial in high-stakes marketing. This is where AI emerges as the ultimate analyst, diving into marketing campaigns' performance data to unearth insights that can drive future success. It's about turning hindsight into foresight, learning from every click and conversion to refine and optimize.

- AI tools track the performance of various marketing channels, from social media to email, analyzing everything from engagement rates to conversion paths. This analysis isn't just descriptive; it's predictive, offering a glimpse into how tweaks and changes might improve outcomes.
- By correlating specific actions with results, AI helps marketers understand the true ROI of their efforts, guiding them on where to invest their resources for the best returns.

This meticulous analysis ensures that marketing is not just an art but a science, one where every decision is informed, every strategy is tested, and every dollar spent is an investment in future success.

In the dynamic marketing world, AI is not just a tool; it's a revolution, transforming how we connect, engage, and persuade. It's personalization at a scale never seen before, where every message is a bridge, every piece of content a handshake, and every campaign a conversation. In this new era, AI is the compass guiding marketers through the uncharted waters of consumer preferences, ensuring that no effort is wasted and every connection counts.

Financial Forecasting and Risk Management

In the ever-evolving finance landscape, where unpredictability is the only constant, generative AI emerges as a beacon of insight and assurance. It sifts through the chaos of market data, draws patterns from the past, and illuminates the path ahead, offering businesses and individuals a clearer view of their financial futures.

Market Analysis

Navigating the financial markets involves tracking economic indicators, corporate earnings reports, and geopolitical events. AI can help by analyzing large amounts of market data to predict trends and find investment opportunities. It uses advanced algorithms to detect changes in market sentiment, forecast stock price movements, and anticipate the impact of global events on investments. This capability transforms the approach to investing, making it possible to:

- React swiftly to emerging trends, securing advantageous positions before they become common knowledge.

- Diversify investment portfolios with a data-backed understanding of potential risks and returns, ensuring a more balanced approach to wealth growth.

Risk Assessment

Risk lurks around every corner in the financial world, from the uncertainty of loans to the specter of fraudulent transactions. Generative AI acts as a vigilant guardian, enhancing the ability to assess and mitigate these risks. Analyzing transaction data patterns can identify anomalies that signal potential fraud, enabling preemptive action to safeguard assets. In credit risk management, AI delves into borrowers' financial behaviors and history, offering a nuanced assessment beyond traditional credit scores. This granular analysis supports more informed lending decisions, reducing default rates and fostering a healthier credit environment. Key benefits include:

- Enhanced fraud detection mechanisms that adapt in real-time, keeping pace with fraudsters' evolving tactics.
- A more personalized creditworthiness assessment opens doors for those who conventional metrics might underserve.

Personalized Financial Advice

In a world where financial advice used to be only for the wealthy, AI is changing the game by providing personalized guidance to everyone. It interprets individual financial situations, goals, and risk tolerances, crafting personalized advice that spans budgeting, investing, and saving. This isn't about one-off suggestions but an ongoing dialogue where AI continuously refines its guidance based on new data and life changes. Individuals and businesses benefit from:

- Investment recommendations that align with personal goals and market conditions dynamically adjust as both evolve.
- Budgeting tools that not only track spending but also offer insights on how to optimize savings and reduce unnecessary expenses.

Regulatory Compliance

The maze of financial regulations is daunting, with new rules constantly emerging and the stakes for noncompliance high. AI offers a map and a compass, simplifying the journey through this complex landscape. It monitors regulatory changes, ensuring businesses can swiftly adapt their operations to remain compliant. More than just a watchdog, AI predicts how upcoming regulations might impact business models and financial products, allowing for proactive adjustments. This foresight is invaluable, enabling:

- A reduction in compliance costs through automated monitoring and reporting processes that eliminate manual errors and inefficiencies.
- The ability to innovate confidently, knowing new products and services are designed with compliance in mind from the outset.

In the intricate dance of finance, where precision and foresight are paramount, generative AI leads with grace. It transforms data into insight, risk into opportunity, and complexity into clarity. Through its lens, the future of finance is not just a tale of numbers but a story of personalized possibilities and informed decisions, where each step forward is made with confidence and understanding.

The Role of AI in Sustainable Practices

AI is a critical player in the green revolution in a world where the balance between progress and the planet is more crucial than ever. It's not just about making businesses more efficient; it's about steering them toward more sustainable paths. Through clever optimization, waste slashing, and the greening of supply chains, AI is not just a tool for growth but a sustainability partner.

Energy Efficiency

In the quest for sustainability, energy consumption is a significant concern for businesses worldwide. AI emerges as a powerful ally, optimizing energy use from factory floors to office spaces. By analyzing patterns of energy consumption and identifying inefficiencies, AI systems can automate adjustments to machinery, lighting, heating, and cooling systems, ensuring that energy is used only when and where it's needed. This isn't just about cutting costs; it's about reducing carbon footprints and contributing to a more sustainable future. For example, smart buildings equipped with AI can adapt to changes in occupancy and weather, maintaining comfort while minimizing energy waste.

Waste Reduction

Waste is an inevitable byproduct of production and consumption, but AI is helping to minimize its impact. Through advanced analytics, AI pinpoints inefficiencies in manufacturing processes that lead to waste, suggesting improvements that conserve materials. In operations, AI-driven sorting systems can more accurately separate recyclable materials, increasing the efficiency of recycling programs. Furthermore, AI models predict demand patterns more accurately, reducing overproduction and excess waste, often resulting in landfills. This approach conserves resources and opens avenues for a circular economy, where waste is minimized, and materials are reused, creating a sustainability loop.

Sustainable Supply Chains

The journey from raw material to finished product is long, and traditionally, it's been opaque. AI introduces transparency and efficiency into this process, ensuring that sustainability isn't just a buzzword but a practice embedded in every step. By analyzing data across the supply chain, AI enables companies to identify suppliers that adhere to sustainable practices, from reducing emissions to ensuring fair labor conditions. Moreover, AI can optimize logistics, reducing the carbon footprint associated with transportation. These intelligent networks are not just about streamlining operations; they are committed to ethical and environmental standards.

Environmental Monitoring

Beyond the confines of businesses and industries, AI extends its reach into the very heart of conservation efforts. It monitors ecosystems and wildlife, providing data crucial for preserving biodiversity. Drones and satellite images, analyzed by AI, track changes in land use, deforestation, and the health of natural habitats. Similarly, AI algorithms process sounds from remote sensors to monitor wildlife populations and detect illegal logging or poaching activities. This wide net of surveillance and analysis is vital for timely interventions and long-term conservation planning, ensuring our progress doesn't come at the planet's expense.

As this chapter draws close, we're reminded that AI's potential extends beyond economic growth and efficiency. It's a vital ally in the quest for sustainability, offering solutions that balance human needs with the health of our planet. From optimizing energy use to reducing waste, greening supply chains, and monitoring the environment, AI is at the forefront of the green revolution, proving that technology and sustainability can go hand in hand. As we move forward, integrating AI into sustainable practices offers a blueprint for a future where progress doesn't compromise the planet.

Moving on, let's explore how these technological advancements in AI are not just reshaping businesses and environmental efforts but also redefining the very fabric of society.

FIVE

Navigating the Ethical Maze of Generative AI

Imagine you're at a crossroads. One path leads to AI amplifying our biases, and the other to a future where technology champions fairness and inclusion. This isn't just a thought experiment; it's the natural choice facing us in developing and deploying generative AI. As we stand at this junction, our decisions will shape the technology itself and the society it serves.

Bias and Fairness in AI Algorithms

Identifying Bias

Bias in AI algorithms is like a mirror reflecting the prejudices and assumptions ingrained in our data and, by extension, our society. It sneaks in through skewed data sets—collections of information that don't accurately represent the real world's diversity. Imagine training a facial recognition system solely on images of people from a single ethnicity; it's bound to stumble when faced with anyone outside that narrow dataset. Likewise, developer prejudices, even unintentional, can color the algorithms we create, subtly directing them to favor specific outcomes over others.

Impact on Society

When AI systems inherit our biases, they can perpetuate and amplify them, reinforcing stereotypes and deepening inequalities. It's a scenario where a job recruitment tool prefers male candidates for technical roles because it was trained on historical hiring data that skewed male. Or a credit-scoring AI that disadvantages certain ethnic groups because it mirrors past discriminatory lending practices. Each of these instances shows how AI, left unchecked, can serve to entrench societal divides rather than bridge them.

Mitigation Strategies

The fight against bias in AI is multifaceted, requiring vigilance at every step of the development process. Here are some proven, practical strategies:

- **Diverse Data Sets**: Ensuring that the data used to train AI systems represents a broad spectrum of humanity is crucial. This means including various ethnicities, genders, ages, and more to give AI a complete picture of the world it serves.
- **Team Inclusivity**: The teams behind AI systems should be as diverse as the audiences they aim to serve. Various perspectives can help identify potential biases and blind spots in AI development.
- **Regular Audits**: AI systems should undergo regular checks for biased outcomes, especially in high-stakes areas like healthcare or law enforcement. These audits can be internal or, ideally, performed by independent third parties to ensure accountability.

- **Feedback Loops**: Encouraging users to report biased outcomes or errors provides valuable data that can help refine and correct AI systems. This feedback loop creates a dynamic system that evolves and improves over time.

Case Studies

Real-world examples highlight challenges and solutions in addressing AI bias:

- In one instance, a major tech company found its AI-powered hiring tool favored male candidates. The discovery led to the tool's discontinuation and a renewed focus on developing more equitable AI solutions.
- Another case involved a facial recognition system used by law enforcement that was significantly less accurate in identifying people of color. Public outcry and legal challenges prompted a reevaluation of the technology's use and the development of more precise, less biased systems.

These case studies underscore the importance of vigilance and continuous improvement in the quest to build AI systems that serve all of society equitably. They remind us that technology, at its best, is a tool for amplifying our highest ideals, not our worst prejudices.

As we navigate the ethical maze of generative AI, our choices will determine tomorrow's landscape. It's a journey filled with challenges and immense potential for positive change. By committing to fairness, inclusivity, and continuous learning, we can ensure that AI becomes a force for good, breaking down barriers and opening up new horizons for everyone.

Privacy Concerns in the Age of AI

In this digital age, where every click, search, and interaction leaves a digital footprint, privacy concerns have moved from the periphery to the center stage of the AI discussion. AI systems are traders in a world where personal information is the currency. The ethical implications of AI's insatiable appetite for data are vast, touching on consent, transparency, and the fine line between personalization and intrusion.

Data Collection and Use

At the heart of the privacy debate is how AI systems gather and utilize personal data. These systems feed on information, using it to learn, adapt, and, ultimately, serve us better. But there's a catch. This data often includes sensitive information that, if mishandled, could lead to unintended consequences. For instance, health apps that track your physical activity and dietary habits could, without proper safeguards, inadvertently expose your medical conditions. The ethical challenge lies in ensuring that AI systems respect the sanctity of personal data, using it to enhance lives without compromising privacy.

- **Data Anonymization**: One approach to safeguarding privacy is data anonymization, which strips away identifiers that link data to individuals. While this doesn't make the data entirely anonymous, it adds a layer of protection, making it harder to trace back to individuals.
- **Minimal Data Use**: Another strategy is for AI systems to collect only the data necessary for their function, avoiding the temptation to hoard information "just in case." This principle of data minimization is crucial to building trust and ensuring privacy.

Consent and Transparency

Consent and transparency are the twin pillars upon which the ethical use of AI rests. Users have the right to know what data is being collected, for what purpose, and how it's used. More importantly, they should be able to opt in or out, making informed decisions about their digital footprints. Precise, understandable consent mechanisms are critical, moving from lengthy, jargon-filled terms of service to concise, straightforward explanations.

- **Granular Consent Options**: Instead of a single, blanket consent for all data uses, AI systems could offer users choices about what data they're comfortable sharing and for what purposes.
- **Ongoing Consent**: Consent isn't just a one-time checkbox but an ongoing process. As AI systems evolve and data use changes, users should be able to revisit and revise their consent choices.

Protective Measures

Various protective measures have been implemented technologically and legislatively in response to growing privacy concerns. The General Data Protection Regulation (GDPR) in the European Union stands as a beacon of comprehensive privacy legislation, setting stringent standards for data protection and user rights. It embodies principles of consent, data minimization, and transparency, serving as a model for other regions.

- **Encryption and Secure Storage**: Beyond legislation, technological solutions like encryption ensure that data, even if accessed, remains unreadable to unauthorized

parties. Secure storage protects against breaches, keeping sensitive information from falling into the wrong hands.
- **AI Ethics Boards**: Many organizations have established ethics boards to oversee AI development, ensuring that privacy considerations are woven into the fabric of AI systems from the ground up.

Balancing Act

Balancing the use of AI for innovation while protecting individual privacy rights is like walking a tightrope. On one side, there's the drive to personalize and make AI systems as helpful and intuitive as possible. On the other hand, there's the imperative to protect and ensure that this personalization doesn't come at the cost of personal privacy. It's a delicate balance, demanding a nuanced approach that respects individual rights while embracing the benefits of AI.

- **Privacy by Design**: Incorporating privacy into the very architecture of AI systems, rather than as an afterthought, is critical. This approach ensures that privacy considerations guide the development process, from data collection to user interaction.
- **User Empowerment**: Ultimately, empowering users to manage their data is crucial to understanding and controlling its use. Tools that provide insights into data collection and usage, along with easy-to-use privacy settings, put the power back in the hands of users, making privacy a shared responsibility.

In this digital innovation landscape, where AI systems learn from and adapt to our behaviors, navigating privacy concerns is an ethical imperative and a foundational aspect of trust. It's about creating an environment where technology serves humanity without compromising the values we hold dear. As we move forward, weaving these threads of concern, consent, protection, and balance into the fabric of AI development is not just wise but essential.

Ethical Design and Development Practices

Creating ethical guidelines is essential in the constantly changing world of generative AI. Accountability, transparency, and fairness are the key principles that ensure we develop AI with integrity and trust.

Principles of Ethical AI

- **Accountability**: This principle ensures that there's always a clear line of responsibility for AI's decisions and actions. It's about creating systems where it's always possible to pinpoint who or what is accountable for the outcomes of AI, ensuring that there's recourse for errors or harm.
- **Transparency**: The goal is to make AI's decision-making process understandable to those who use it and those impacted by its decisions. This involves detailing how data is used and how decisions are made and providing this information in a way that's accessible and understandable.
- **Fairness**: Ensuring AI treats all users equally, without inherent bias or discrimination, is crucial. This means actively eliminating biases in datasets and algorithms and striving for equitable outcomes across diverse user groups.

Incorporating Ethics in the AI Lifecycle

Integrating ethical considerations into every stage of AI development is beneficial; it's crucial for building trust and ensuring technology's positive impact on society. Ethics play a role throughout the AI lifecycle:

- **Design Phase**: At the outset, ethical AI means setting clear objectives that align with societal values and norms. It involves engaging with diverse stakeholders to understand the broad implications of the technology being developed.
- **Development Phase**: As the AI system takes shape, continuously testing for biases, ensuring data privacy, and maintaining transparency about data sources and algorithms become vital practices.
- **Deployment Phase**: When AI systems go live, maintaining an open channel for feedback and criticism allows for the ongoing refinement of ethical practices. Monitoring the system in real-world scenarios ensures it operates as intended without causing unforeseen harm.

Role of Ethicists in AI

Including ethicists in AI development teams marks a significant shift toward more conscientious technology creation. These professionals bring a nuanced understanding of ethical theory and practice, helping to navigate the complex moral landscape of AI. Their role involves:

- **Guiding Ethical Decision-Making**: Ethicists help identify potential ethical issues before they arise, offering strategies to mitigate risks and ensure equitable outcomes.

- **Educating Teams**: Ethicists foster a culture of responsibility and integrity among developers and engineers by sharing insights into the importance of ethics in AI.
- **Acting as Advocates**: In discussions about new projects or features, ethicists advocate for user rights and ethical principles, ensuring they're central to the development process.

Emerging Standards and Frameworks

As generative AI advances, various standards and frameworks are emerging to promote ethical AI practices. These guidelines serve as a blueprint for developers, providing a structured approach to ethical AI creation. Some of the most notable include:

- **IEEE's Ethically Aligned Design**: A comprehensive set of recommendations that guide AI developers in prioritizing ethical considerations, focusing on human rights, well-being, and accountability.
- **EU's Ethics Guidelines for Trustworthy AI**: This framework outlines seven critical requirements for ethical AI, including transparency, diversity, and environmental well-being, offering a roadmap for compliance with European values and regulations.
- **Partnership on AI's Tenets**: Created by a consortium of tech companies and academic institutions, these tenets advocate for AI that benefits people and society, emphasizing safety, fairness, and accountability.

Each of these frameworks contributes to a growing consensus on the importance of ethics in AI, offering practical steps for integrating these principles into the development process. They represent a collective effort to ensure that AI serves humanity's best interests, respects our rights, enhances our well-being, and enriches our societies.

Ethical design and practices are key in developing generative AI to create powerful and responsible technology. We can ensure AI is innovative, respectful, and protective by focusing on accountability, transparency, and fairness and involving ethicists. New standards and frameworks help us develop AI that aligns with our core values and goals.

The Future of Employment and AI

The dialogue around AI's role in the job market often swings between utopian and dystopian narratives. However, the reality lies in the nuanced shades between these extremes. AI's influence unfolds in complex yet ultimately hopeful ways.

Job Displacement Concerns

The specter of job displacement looms large in discussions about AI and automation. There's a palpable fear that machines capable of performing tasks with incredible speed, accuracy, and cost-efficiency than humans will render many jobs obsolete. This concern isn't unfounded. Specific sectors, particularly those involving repetitive or routine tasks, are already witnessing this shift. It's a trend that demands attention, not just for the economic implications but for the societal impact of rising unemployment rates in affected industries. Yet, this challenge also presents an opportunity for reflection and recalibration regarding the value and nature of work in our lives.

New Job Creation

Conversely, AI's ascendance is not a zero-sum game. History teaches us that technological advancements, while disrupting existing job markets, also pave the way for new opportunities. AI is no exception, fostering entirely new job categories and industries. The landscape is evolving from AI ethicists to data scientists, from AI integration specialists to user experience designers for AI systems. These roles, many of which didn't exist a decade ago, underscore AI's potential to displace, create and diversify employment opportunities. This evolution, however, hinges on our ability to anticipate and prepare for the demands of a new AI-integrated job market.

- **Skill Adaptation and Retraining**: The key to navigating this transition is emphasizing upskilling and retraining. The workforce must adapt to the changing landscape, acquiring the skills necessary to thrive alongside AI. Initiatives ranging from coding boot camps to AI literacy programs in traditional education systems are pivotal. They represent the bridges connecting the current workforce to future opportunities, ensuring that the rise of AI is not a tale of displacement but of adaptation and growth.

Evolving Workforce Dynamics

AI is changing the "what" of work and the "how." Remote work capabilities, accelerated by global events, have benefited immensely from AI's advancements. From project management tools that optimize workflows to AI-driven platforms facilitating collaboration across time zones, the integration of AI is making the workplace more flexible and interconnected. Furthermore, the emergence of human-AI collaboration presents a frontier brimming with potential. In creative industries, for example, AI tools that automate the tedious aspects of design free up human creativity for higher-level conceptual thinking. Such synergies enhance productivity and enrich the work, making it more creative and fulfilling.

- **Human-AI Collaboration**: This partnership between humans and AI systems is predicated on the understanding that AI can augment human abilities, not replace them. It's a collaborative future where AI handles data analysis at scale while humans bring the nuanced judgment and creative spark. Preparing for this future means reimagining education and training to equip individuals with the skills to leverage AI, foster a tech-savvy workforce, and be adept at working alongside intelligent systems.

Policy and Support Systems

Navigating AI's transformative impact on employment necessitates proactive policy interventions and robust support systems. Governments, educational institutions, and businesses must collaborate to create an ecosystem that supports workforce transitions in an AI-driven economy.

- **Educational Reform**: Curricula must evolve to include AI literacy, critical thinking, and problem-solving skills from an early age. This foundation will prepare future generations for a job market inextricably linked with AI and technology.
- **Lifelong Learning**: Beyond formal education, fostering a culture of lifelong learning is essential. Access to continuous education and upskilling opportunities will

enable workers to remain agile and adaptable as the job market evolves.
- **Social Safety Nets**: Reinforcing social safety nets for those affected by automation-driven displacement is crucial. Policies that support income, retraining, and job placement can ease the transition, ensuring that the benefits of AI are broadly shared across society.
- **Public-Private Partnerships**: Collaboration between the public and private sectors can drive the development of training programs, incentivize the creation of new jobs in emerging industries, and ensure that the workforce is prepared for the future job market. These partnerships can also play a key role in funding research and innovation in AI, further expanding the frontier of job opportunities.

In the complex world of AI's impact on jobs, it's not about inevitable obsolescence but rather about discovering new opportunities. It's a future where AI acts as both catalyst and companion in the evolution of work, challenging us to reimagine our roles and aspirations in an interconnected world. As we navigate this transition, our focus must remain on harnessing AI's potential to enrich, rather than diminish, the human experience of work, fostering a resilient, dynamic, and inclusive economy.

Regulation and Governance of AI Technologies

With AI technologies advancing so quickly, navigating the complex world of regulation and governance feels like dealing with a constantly changing maze. Around the globe, countries are grappling with how to create legal frameworks that protect citizens and encourage innovation. The current regulatory landscape is a patchwork of national and international guidelines, reflecting diverse approaches to AI's challenges.

Current Regulatory Landscape

Globally, the approach to AI regulation varies widely. Some countries, recognizing the transformative power of AI, have opted for light-touch regulation to foster innovation. Others, prioritizing privacy and ethical considerations, have implemented more stringent controls. For instance, the European Union's General Data Protection Regulation (GDPR) sets a high bar for data protection, impacting AI development and deployment. Meanwhile, countries like the United States have taken a more decentralized approach, with specific industries and states setting their standards.

Challenges in AI Regulation

Regulating AI is fraught with challenges, not least because of the pace of advancement in technology. Laws and regulations, traditionally slow to change, struggle to keep up with the rapid development cycles of AI technologies. Moreover, the global nature of AI complicates regulatory efforts. Technologies developed in one country can easily cross borders, making it difficult to enforce national regulations. Additionally, there's the issue of technological complexity. The intricate workings of AI systems, particularly those based on machine learning and deep learning, can be opaque, making it hard to apply traditional regulatory frameworks.

Proposed Models for AI Governance

In response to these challenges, several models for AI governance have emerged, each aiming to balance the needs for innovation, protection, and ethical considerations:

- **Multi-Stakeholder Approaches**: These models unite governments, industry leaders, academia, and civil society to develop and enforce AI regulations collaboratively. This approach ensures a diversity of perspectives and promotes regulations that are both effective and equitable.
- **Flexible Regulatory Frameworks**: Instead of rigid laws, some propose developing flexible frameworks that can adapt to the evolving nature of AI technologies. These frameworks could include complex rules for fundamental rights and ethical principles and soft laws like guidelines and standards for rapidly changing areas.
- **International Cooperation**: Given AI's global reach, international cooperation is critical for creating coherent and effective regulations. This could be international treaties, shared standards, or cooperative enforcement agreements.

The Role of International Cooperation

International cooperation is beneficial and necessary for effective AI regulation. AI technologies do not recognize national boundaries, so countries must work together to establish global norms and standards. Organizations such as the United Nations, the OECD, and the G7 have already begun to lay the groundwork for such cooperation, developing principles and recommendations for AI governance. These efforts aim to ensure that AI technologies are developed and used in ways that respect human rights, promote inclusion, and contribute to the common good.

In navigating the future of AI regulation and governance, we are charting the course for a technology that holds immense promise but poses significant challenges. The key lies in finding the balance between fostering innovation and ensuring that AI serves the public interest. By embracing collaborative, flexible, and internationally coordinated approaches to AI governance, we can create a framework that addresses the challenges and harnesses the opportunities AI presents.

As we close this chapter on AI regulation and governance, we're reminded that the path forward requires careful navigation, balancing innovation with the need for oversight. The conversations and decisions happening today around AI governance will shape the future of technology and the kind of societies we live in. It's a journey that demands our attention, creativity, and commitment to principles that uphold the greater good. Looking ahead, the exploration of AI's impact on our personal lives and social fabric continues, promising insights and challenges as we strive to integrate these advanced technologies into the very heart of human experience.

Generative Artificial Intelligence for Beginners

UNRAVEL THE MYSTERIES OF AI WITH EASE AND CONFIDENCE THROUGH PRACTICAL GUIDES, ETHICAL INSIGHTS AND REAL-WORLD APPLICATIONS

"True joy comes from giving without an expectation of receiving anything in return." - Unknown

Hey there, fantastic reader! We've been on quite the adventure together, haven't we? When I started writing this book, my biggest hope was to turn the mysterious world of AI into something as straightforward as daylight for you.

If you're reading this, we've journeyed through the maze of generative AI together, tackling big ideas, practical tools, and even those tricky ethical questions.

Remember how daunting AI seemed at the start? But look at us now! We've explored how AI is more about being a super-helpful buddy than a scary job-snatcher. It's all about making life more prosperous, letting us humans shine at what we do best.

Now, I've got a small favor to ask. It's something simple but super meaningful.

Imagine there's someone out there just like you were—curious and a bit unsure about diving into AI. They're searching for that perfect starting point but are bombarded with too many options and insufficient guidance. That's where you and your experience with this book come in!

Please share your thoughts on this book with a review. It's a quick and easy way to pass on the torch of knowledge. Your insights could light up the path for someone else, helping them see that understanding AI is totally within their reach.

Here's what your review could do:

- Empower a small business owner to innovate and grow.
- Inspire an aspiring entrepreneur to take that bold first step.
- Motivate someone to bring new ideas to their workplace.
- Help someone transform their life with new knowledge.
- Make someone's dream a reality.

Are you feeling that warm, fuzzy feeling yet? You're just 60 seconds away from spreading many good vibes.

Scan the QR code below and share your journey:

If you're up for making someone's day a little brighter and helping they find their way in the AI world; you're a hero in my book.

Welcome to our community of AI adventurers. You're a true star! I can't wait to continue this journey with you, diving even deeper into the wonders of AI. There are so many more strategies waiting for us in the chapters ahead.

Thank you from the bottom of my heart for joining me on this ride. Let's get back to exploring the incredible world of AI together.

With all my gratitude,

Gwen Taylor

P.S. Did you know sharing a bit of knowledge or encouragement not only helps others grow but also adds a little sparkle to your journey. If this book opened new doors for you, why not pass it on to someone just starting their adventure? Let's keep the cycle of learning and inspiration going!

SIX

AI and the Future of Tomorrow

Imagine waking up to a world where your morning coffee is prepared by an intelligent machine that knows how you like it, thick with cream and a hint of cinnamon. Imagine your daily commute in a self-driving car that smoothly navigates traffic while you relax and catch up on a book. A digital assistant has organized your day at work, prioritizing tasks based on deadlines and your productivity patterns. This isn't a snippet from a sci-fi novel; it's a peek into a not-so-distant future sculpted by generative AI.

AI's Role in Shaping Future Societies

Societal Changes

Generative AI is on track to redefine the very fabric of society, touching everything from how we learn to how we manage our health. In education, imagine platforms that adapt to each student's learning pace, style, and preferences, making "falling behind" a thing of the past. Healthcare sees similar revolutions, with AI predicting illnesses before they manifest, offering a window for preventive measures that could save millions of lives and dollars.

- In cities, AI-driven analytics help manage resources more efficiently, reducing waste and improving the quality of life. Intelligent routing and energy use optimization could minimize traffic congestion and optimize energy use across sprawling urban landscapes.

Opportunities for Improvement

The potential for AI to drive societal improvements is immense. It offers solutions to age-old problems like access to quality education and healthcare by removing barriers of geography and socioeconomic status. For example, remote villages could access world-class education and medical advice through AI-powered platforms, leveling the playing field in previously unimaginable ways.

- AI also promises to make our cities more innovative and more sustainable. By analyzing data on energy consumption, traffic patterns, and waste management, AI can help us build urban environments that are livable and truly thriving spaces for future generations.

Potential Pitfalls

However, with great power comes great responsibility. The integration of AI into society has its challenges. One pressing concern is the widening gap in inequality. The benefits of AI could disproportionately favor those with access to cutting-edge technology, leaving others further behind.

- Another concern is privacy. The data they gather increases as AI systems become more embedded in our daily lives. Without stringent safeguards, this could lead to unprecedented levels of surveillance and the erosion of personal freedoms.

Vision for the Future

For AI to truly benefit society, its development and deployment must be guided by ethical principles and a commitment to equity. Imagine a future where AI tools are designed not just by a tech-savvy few but in collaboration with communities around the globe. This inclusive approach ensures that AI solutions address various needs and challenges, from rural education to urban sustainability.

- A future society shaped by AI could minimize everyday inconveniences, leaving more room for human creativity, empathy, and exploration. It's a world where technology takes care of the mundane, empowering us to live our lives to the fullest.

Visual Element: Infographic on AI in Daily Life

An infographic titled "A Day in the Life: AI Edition" visually depicts how generative AI integrates into every aspect of a typical day, from personalized news feeds in the morning to AI-driven health monitoring before bed. It highlights key areas of impact: education, Healthcare, urban living, and Personal Privacy, offering a glimpse into a day fueled by intelligent technology.

Interactive Element: AI Readiness Quiz

A short quiz titled "How AI-Ready Are You?" helps readers assess their understanding and preparedness for the AI-driven future. Questions range from basic knowledge about AI to opinions on ethical considerations and privacy concerns, offering personalized tips based on results.

Textual Element: Checklist for Ethical AI Usage

A downloadable checklist guides individuals and businesses on ethically incorporating AI into their operations. It includes points like:

- Verify the sources of your AI tools.
- Regularly audit AI systems for bias.
- Ensure transparency in AI-driven decisions.
- Foster ongoing dialogue about AI ethics within your organization.

By embedding generative AI into the very essence of our daily lives, we stand at the threshold of a new era. One where the tapestries of our societies are woven with threads of intelligent technology, promising a future that's not only more efficient but more equitable. The path forward is laden with challenges, but with a vigilant focus on ethics, privacy, and inclusivity, the potential for AI to enrich our lives is boundless. As we enter this new dawn, the choices we make today will set the foundation for the societies of tomorrow, ensuring that we harness the power of AI not just for the few but for all.

Creativity and AI: Collaboration or Competition?

In the ever-evolving landscape of art and innovation, AI tools have emerged not as rivals in the age-old pursuit of creativity but as allies, offering fresh avenues for artistic expression. The synergy between human imagination and algorithmic precision opens a world where the boundaries of creativity continually expand, challenging our preconceptions of what it means to create.

Augmenting Human Creativity

The fusion of AI with human creativity has given birth to breathtakingly novel forms of art and design, music composition, and storytelling. AI tools, with their ability to process vast datasets and identify patterns invisible to the human eye, provide artists with a unique palette from which to work. For instance, musicians can now collaborate with AI to compose complex pieces, blending traditional elements with sounds the human mind might not conceive independently. Similarly, visual artists utilize AI to merge styles across periods, creating stunning visuals that carry the essence of the past while firmly rooted in the present.

- AI's contribution to creative processes often involves the heavy lifting of data analysis, allowing artists to focus on the essence of their work. This partnership has created dynamic art installations that interact with viewers in real time, adapting and evolving based on audience reactions.

Concerns about Originality

Despite the exciting prospects, the rise of AI in creative domains has sparked a debate around originality and authenticity. Skeptics argue that art generated by algorithms lacks the depth and emotion that come from the human experience. The crux of this concern lies in whether AI can be creative or merely replicate and remix human-generated content.

- To address these concerns, it's vital to recognize AI's role as a tool in the artist's kit, like a brush or a camera. The essence of creativity, the spark that ignites a piece of art, remains human. AI-generated works often undergo a curatorial process, where artists imbue them with meaning, context, and personal touch, ensuring that the final piece resonates on a human level.

Collaborative Projects

Collaborative projects between artists and AI show how they can work together, enhancing human creativity rather than taking away from it. These collaborations have yielded projects that challenge our perceptions of art and its creation. For example, filmmakers are experimenting with AI to script narratives that adapt based on viewer responses, creating an immersive, interactive storytelling experience. In the visual arts, AI algorithms trained on specific artists' styles can collaborate with living artists to create hybrid works that dialogue between the creator and the creation.

- Successful collaborations often hinge on the artist's ability to guide the AI, setting parameters and molds for the AI to fill with its algorithmic creativity. This partnership underscores the notion that AI in the creative process is a medium, not the message.

Future of Creative Professions

As we look to the future, integrating AI into creative professions suggests a landscape ripe with opportunity. Far from rendering artists obsolete, AI stands to remove the struggle from the creative process, automating tasks like color correction in photography or sound mixing in music production. This liberation from the technical minutiae allows creators to devote more time to the heart of their work: innovation, experimentation, and emotional depth.

- The role of creativity in an AI-enhanced world shifts toward conceptual thinking, strategy, and interpretation. Artists and creatives become orchestrators, guiding AI to execute visions that might be beyond human capability alone. This evolution doesn't diminish human creativity's value. Still, it redefines it, emphasizing aspects like creativity, emotional intelligence, and contextual understanding—qualities AI cannot replicate.

We don't see a conflict but a rich collaboration in the dynamic relationship between human creativity and AI. The relationship is not one of competition but of mutual enhancement, where each brings strengths that complement the other. As AI continues to evolve, its role in the creative process promises to expand the horizons of what we consider possible, inviting us to reimagine the act of creation itself. In this journey, the essence of art remains unchanged: a reflection of the human condition, a dialogue between creator and observer, mediated by the tools of our times. As we move forward, blending AI into this dialogue introduces a new vocabulary that speaks to the endless potential of human and machine collaboration.

The Digital Divide and Access to AI

Imagine two worlds coexisting side by side. AI is a daily reality, enhancing lives, streamlining work, and opening new vistas of creativity. In contrast, this technology remains a distant dream, accessible only in snippets through overheard conversations or glimpsed on the screens of the more fortunate. This isn't a scene from a futuristic novel but a reflection of today's digital divide. This rift separates those with access to digital technologies, including AI, from those without.

Defining the Digital Divide

At its core, the digital divide is unequal access to digital technologies. A gap manifests in physical access to devices and the internet and the skills and knowledge to use these technologies effectively. This divide has profound implications for AI, as access to AI technologies can significantly influence one's ability to learn, work, and engage with society. The gap isn't just digital; it's economic, educational, and social, affecting everything from job opportunities to healthcare outcomes.

Impact on Global Inequality

The uneven distribution of AI technologies can deepen global inequalities, creating a world where some regions leap ahead, harnessing AI for growth and innovation while others fall further behind. This disparity isn't limited to the distinction between developed and developing countries. Within nations, urban areas often have a technological edge over rural ones, and socioeconomic status can significantly influence one's access to AI and digital literacy. The risk is a world where the benefits of AI—its potential to solve complex problems, enhance productivity, and create new forms of art and communication—are unevenly distributed, amplifying existing disparities.

Bridging the Gap

Addressing the digital divide requires a concerted effort across multiple fronts. Some initiatives and strategies show promise:

- **Infrastructure Development**: Building and enhancing digital infrastructure in underserved areas is foundational. This means laying down cables and ensuring reliable and affordable internet access.
- **Education and Training**: Equipping individuals with digital literacy skills is crucial. This involves integrating digital skills into school curricula and providing adult education programs focused on digital literacy and AI awareness.
- **Community Access Points**: Establishing community centers equipped with internet access and digital devices can provide communal entry points to the digital world and serve as hubs for digital literacy training.
- **Affordable Technology**: Making digital devices and AI technologies more affordable can help level the playing field. This could involve partnerships between tech companies and governments to subsidize costs or offer devices at reduced prices to low-income households.
- **Local Content and Language Support**: Ensuring digital content, including AI applications, is available in local languages and relevant to local contexts can increase engagement and utility.

Role of Education and Policy

The twin engines of education and policy are vital in propelling efforts to close the digital divide. Education empowers individuals with the skills to navigate the digital world and fosters a deeper understanding of how AI can be used responsibly and ethically. Conversely, policy can set the framework for equitable access by promoting initiatives that prioritize digital inclusion and address barriers to access. Together, education and policy can create an environment where digital technologies and AI become tools for empowerment rather than instruments of division.

- **Curriculum Integration**: Incorporating digital literacy and AI education into school curricula ensures that students are prepared to engage with technology critically and creatively from a young age.
- **Teacher Training**: Equipping teachers with the skills and knowledge to integrate digital technologies and AI into their teaching practices is essential for effective education.
- **Inclusive Policy Frameworks**: Developing policies that specifically target the reduction of the digital divide, from funding for digital infrastructure to programs that support digital literacy, ensures a coordinated approach to digital inclusion.
- **Public-Private Partnerships**: Collaborations between governments, tech companies, and nonprofits can harness the strengths of each sector to address the digital divide more effectively. These partnerships can focus on everything from infrastructure development to educational programs and affordable access to technology.

In a world increasingly shaped by AI, ensuring equitable access to this transformative technology is more than a matter of digital convenience; it's a question of social justice and economic opportunity. We can bridge the digital divide through targeted initiatives and strategic collaborations, creating a future where all share AI's benefits, not just the privileged few. By doing this, we improve people's lives and enhance our global society, bringing together innovation, inclusion, and progress.

AI and Its Impact on Privacy and Security

The digital age has brought us to a critical crossroads. The marvels of AI technologies promise a safer world, yet paradoxically, they also present unprecedented risks to our privacy. This dichotomy invites us to tread carefully, ensuring that as we bolster our defenses against digital threats, we do not unwittingly erode the very liberties we seek to protect.

Enhancing Security

AI's prowess in enhancing security measures is undeniable. Its ability to sift through vast datasets swiftly and identify patterns invisible to the human eye makes it an invaluable ally in cybersecurity and fraud detection. For instance, in cybersecurity, AI algorithms are trained to detect anomalies in network traffic, identifying potential threats such as malware and phishing attacks before they can cause harm. Similarly, in fraud detection, AI systems analyze transaction data in real time, flagging activities that deviate from established patterns, such as unusual purchase locations or amounts, thereby preventing financial loss before it occurs.

- Automated threat detection enables organizations to respond rapidly and efficiently to cybersecurity threats.
- Real-time transaction monitoring significantly reduces the window of opportunity for fraudulent activities, safeguarding both businesses and customers from financial harm.

Privacy at Risk

However, the capabilities that make AI an asset in security can also, if misused, turn it into a tool for invasive surveillance and privacy breaches. The depth and breadth of personal data AI systems require to function effectively can, in the wrong hands, become a blueprint for intrusive monitoring of individuals' activities and behaviors. For example, facial recognition technology, powered by AI, can enhance security in public spaces but also raise ethical concerns when used for mass surveillance without explicit consent, blurring the line between safety and privacy invasion.

- The accumulation of personal data by AI systems raises questions about who can access this information and how it is used.
- The potential misuse of AI for intrusive monitoring poses a significant threat to individual freedoms and privacy.

Ethical Security Practices

Adopting ethical practices in using AI for security applications is paramount to navigating these choppy waters. This means ensuring transparency in how AI systems operate and the data they collect, obtaining informed consent from individuals whose data is being processed, and implementing strict data protection measures to prevent unauthorized access. Moreover, there should be clear guidelines on the acceptable use of AI in surveillance, emphasizing respect for individual privacy and human rights.

- Transparency about the data collected by AI systems and its intended use helps build trust and ensures individuals know how their information is utilized.
- Informed consent protocols ensure individuals can choose whether or not their data is used by AI systems, respecting their autonomy and privacy rights.

Navigating the Privacy-Security Balance

Striking a balance between leveraging AI for security and safeguarding individual privacy requires a multifaceted approach. One key strategy is the data minimization principle, which advocates collecting only the data necessary for a specific security purpose. This approach reduces the risk of privacy breaches. It streamlines the data analysis, focusing AI's efforts on genuinely relevant information.

- Employing end-to-end encryption for data collected by AI systems adds a layer of security, ensuring that even if data is intercepted, it remains unintelligible to unauthorized parties.
- Regular audits of AI systems by independent evaluators can help identify and rectify potential privacy vulnerabilities, ensuring that security measures do not infringe upon individual rights.

Moreover, it is crucial to foster an ongoing dialogue between technologists, policymakers, and the public about the ethical use of AI in security. These conversations can lead to developing robust regulatory frameworks that protect public safety and privacy. Additionally, investing in public education about digital security and privacy rights empowers individuals to make informed decisions about their data, further strengthening the privacy-security nexus.

- Developing clear regulatory frameworks that define the boundaries of AI use in security applications can help prevent abuses and ensure accountability.
- Public education initiatives raise awareness about digital privacy rights and the responsible use of

technology, fostering a more informed and vigilant society.

In this era of digital sophistication, where AI holds the key to unprecedented security capabilities, we find ourselves navigating a complex landscape. The path forward demands a delicate balance, harnessing AI's potential to protect and defend while steadfastly guarding the sanctity of our private lives. As we continue to explore AI's vast possibilities, our compass remains fixed on the principles of ethics, transparency, and respect for individual rights, guiding us through the challenges and opportunities.

Preparing for an AI-Enhanced Future

In an era rapidly reshaped by generative AI, the ability to adapt and thrive amid change is paramount. This readiness isn't just about grasping the nuts and bolts of technology but about fostering a mindset that welcomes transformation, sees potential in challenges, and eagerly participates in crafting the future.

Readiness for Change

Embracing AI's transformative power begins with a shift in perspective, viewing changes not as hurdles but as stepping stones to progress. Education systems play a pivotal role, evolving to impart knowledge about AI's mechanics and cultivate adaptability, critical thinking, and ethical reasoning. This holistic approach ensures that, as the workforce transitions into AI-integrated roles, individuals are technically prepared and mentally agile, ready to navigate and shape the shifting landscape of work and society.

- Lifelong learning emerges as a critical theme, highlighting the importance of continuous skill development. It's about creating learning ecosystems that support individuals at all stages of their careers and encourage them to grow with technology.

Inclusive AI Development

For AI to truly benefit everyone, its development must consider the diverse experiences of all people. This inclusivity means bringing diverse voices to the table and ensuring that AI solutions are designed with a broad spectrum of needs and perspectives in mind. It's about recognizing that the most effective and equitable AI systems are those forged through collaboration across cultures, disciplines, and communities.

- Engaging underrepresented groups in AI development mitigates the risk of biased algorithms and opens doors to innovative solutions that address wide-ranging societal challenges. It's a call to action for developers, policymakers, and the public to champion diversity in the AI field.

Public Engagement and Awareness

The future of AI is not just in the hands of tech giants and innovators but also in society's collective imagination and participation. Public engagement and awareness initiatives demystify AI, breaking down barriers of understanding and fear. Through open dialogues, workshops, and media, the mysteries of AI unfold into opportunities for everyone to contribute their insights and ideas.

- This public discourse fosters a society aware of AI's potential and vigilant about its ethical use, privacy implications, and social impact. It's a proactive stance, inviting individuals to be part of the conversation and the solution.

Policy and Ethical Frameworks

Robust policy and ethical frameworks that guide AI's development and integration into society are at the foundation of an AI-enhanced future. These frameworks are the guardrails that ensure AI advancements drive progress without compromising our values or well-being. Crafting these policies requires a delicate balance that fosters innovation while safeguarding against misuse, bias, and inequality.

- Developing these frameworks is a dynamic process that evolves with technology and our understanding of its implications. It underscores the need for ongoing research, cross-sector collaboration, and public input to shape effective policies that reflect societal values.

As we stand at the brink of a new era marked by AI's profound influence on our lives, the road ahead beckons with promise and challenges. Our readiness for change, commitment to inclusivity, engagement with the public, and dedication to ethical governance are the compass points guiding us toward a future where AI enhances our world in meaningful, equitable ways. These principles form the bedrock upon which we build not just a technologically advanced society but one richer in understanding, more vibrant in diversity, and unwavering in its commitment to the common good.

As we turn the page, let's carry forward the lessons learned and insights gained, ever mindful of AI's incredible potential to enrich our lives. Together, we step into a future vibrant with possibility, ready to navigate its complexities and harness its opportunities for the benefit of all.

SEVEN

Unlocking Generative AI Tools for Everyone

Picture this: You're standing at the edge of a vast, unexplored digital landscape. It's buzzing with possibilities, tools, and technologies that promise to transform your creative and professional projects. Now, imagine you've got a map in your hands that can guide you through this terrain, showing you where to find the hidden treasures. This chapter is a map designed to navigate the rich world of generative AI tools that cater to myriad needs, from crafting digital art to deciphering data patterns.

Generative AI tools are reshaping how we approach tasks, turning the complex into the manageable and the mundane into the fascinating. But with so many options available, where do you start? Let's walk through the landscape together, highlighting the tools that stand out for their ability to open up new possibilities, their ease of use, and the support they offer to users like you.

Diverse Tools for Various Needs

Generative AI isn't just one-size-fits-all. It's a spectrum of tools designed with specific capabilities:

- Artists and designers can use tools like DALL-E to transform textual descriptions into stunning visuals to blur the lines between imagination and reality.
- Writers can leverage GPT-4-based platforms to turn a rough outline into a compelling narrative or break through the dreaded writer's block.
- Data enthusiasts and business professionals might gravitate toward AI like TensorFlow or IBM Watson. These AIs can analyze trends and make predictions, turning raw data into actionable insights.

Accessibility and User-Friendliness

Remember the first time you tried to ride a bike? It likely felt daunting until you found the right one that clicked. Finding an AI tool can feel similar. The trick is in discovering tools that don't just perform well but are also easy to get into. Here's what to look for:

- **Intuitive interfaces** that guide you rather than confuse you. Think of platforms that offer drag-and-drop functionalities or simple, clean dashboards.
- **Step-by-step tutorials** that guide you through your first projects. These can be video guides, FAQs, or interactive demos.
- **Flexible settings** allow you to tweak the tool's functionalities to your comfort level, gradually exploring more complex features as you gain confidence.

Community Support and Resources

Have you ever been stuck on a video game level, only to find the solution in a forum or walkthrough video? The power of community is undeniable, and it's a critical support system for navigating generative AI tools.

- Look for tools that boast active online forums or user communities—places where you can ask questions, share experiences, and find inspiration.
- Check if the tool has a repository of user-generated templates, scripts, or projects. These can serve as a launching pad for your creations and offer insights into what's possible with the tool.
- Look for regular workshops or webinars hosted by the tool's creators or expert users. These sessions can provide a deep dive into specific features or techniques.

Comparative Overview

Choosing the right generative AI tool is like picking the perfect ingredient for a recipe—it can make all the difference in the result. Here's a brief comparison to get you started:

- **For Visual Creativity**: DALL-E offers unparalleled capacity for generating images from text descriptions, making it ideal for artists and designers looking for inspiration or to bring their wildest ideas to life. On the other hand, Artbreeder allows for blending images, offering a more collaborative approach to creativity.
- **For Writing and Content Creation**: GPT-3 stands out for its ability to generate human-like text, making it a go-to for writers and content creators. Simplified platforms like ShortlyAI and Writesonic provide more user-friendly interfaces, catering to those who may not be tech-savvy but still wish to leverage AI in their writing.
- **For Data Analysis and Business Applications**: TensorFlow's open-source library offers extensive resources for deep-diving into machine learning projects.

IBM Watson provides a more guided experience, with tools tailored for business use cases, including customer service bots and market analysis.

Choosing a generative AI tool doesn't have to be daunting. By considering your specific needs, seeking out user-friendly interfaces, tapping into community resources, and comparing your options, you can find the right tool to unlock new levels of creativity and efficiency in your work. Remember, these tools serve your imagination and ambition, streamlining the journey from idea to reality.

Step-by-Step Guide to Using ChatGPT

Navigating the waters of generative AI can be thrilling and overwhelming for newcomers. ChatGPT is among the standout tools that have captured the imagination of users worldwide. This AI, known for its conversational prowess, can aid in many tasks, from drafting emails to generating creative stories. Here's how you can make ChatGPT your ally in creativity and productivity:

Getting Started with ChatGPT

Initiating your adventure with ChatGPT requires a few simple steps. First, access the platform that hosts ChatGPT. This might be through a website or an app, depending on what's most convenient for you. Once there, you'll likely need to sign up or log in, providing essential information to create an account.

After you're logged in, you'll find yourself at the main interface, where you can start interacting with ChatGPT. Typically, it's as straightforward as typing in a prompt or question and hitting enter. ChatGPT will then process your input and respond like a human in a text conversation. The beauty of ChatGPT lies in its flexibility; there's no one way to use it. Whether you're looking for assistance with a specific task or want to explore its capabilities, simply typing in your request is enough to get started.

Creative and Practical Uses

ChatGPT's versatility makes it a valuable tool for creative and practical endeavors. Creatively, it can act as a brainstorming partner, offering ideas for stories, scripts, or even music lyrics. Writers can use it to flesh out plot outlines or develop character backstories. At the same time, marketers might leverage it for catchy taglines or content ideas.

On the practical side, ChatGPT can simplify life in many ways. It can compose professional emails, draft reports, or summarize articles and papers, saving you significant time. Developers might use it to understand coding concepts or debug issues. At the same time, educators could create custom learning materials tailored to their students' needs.

Tips for Effective Interaction

To get the most out of ChatGPT, consider these strategies for effective interaction:

- **Be Specific**: The more detailed your prompt, the better ChatGPT can tailor its response to meet your needs. Instead of saying, "Write a story," try "About a lost astronaut on Mars."
- **Iterate**: Feel free to refine your prompts based on the responses you get. This is a collaborative process in which each interaction builds on the last.
- **Use Follow-Up Questions**: ChatGPT can maintain the context of a conversation, so feel free to ask follow-up questions for clarification or further information.

Ethical Considerations

While ChatGPT opens up a world of possibilities, navigating its use with an ethical compass is crucial. Here are a few points to remember:

- **Originality and Plagiarism**: When using ChatGPT for content creation, remember that its output is based on existing information. Always ensure that the final work is original and does not infringe on the rights of others.
- **Privacy**: When interacting with ChatGPT, be mindful of sharing sensitive personal information. While reputable platforms have safeguards, it's good practice to avoid disclosing details that could compromise privacy.
- **Responsible Use**: Use ChatGPT in a way that respects the rights and dignity of others. Avoid prompts that could generate harmful or discriminatory content.

Following these guidelines, you can maximize ChatGPT's offerings while fostering a responsible and ethical approach to AI utilization.

Exploring Creative AI with DALL-E

Imagine a tool that turns the wildest fragments of your imagination into visual reality—a digital alchemist that transmutes words into images. This isn't the stuff of fantasy but the groundbreaking reality introduced by DALL-E. This generative AI marvel crafts detailed pictures from textual descriptions. The name, a playful nod to the surreal artist Salvador Dalí and Pixar's lovable robot WALL-E, encapsulates its mission: blending art and technology, bridging human creativity and computational power.

DALL-E operates on a simple yet profound premise: it generates images based on the text inputs it receives. This ability ranges from creating fantastical creatures to visualizing abstract concepts in stunning detail. The tool is not just an artist's companion but a gateway for anyone exploring visual expression's boundaries.

Creative Exploration

Diving into DALL-E is like opening a door to a room where the walls are painted with the colors of your words. Whether you're a seasoned artist looking for inspiration or someone dabbling in creativity for the first time, DALL-E offers a canvas as vast as your imagination. Here are a few ways to spark your creative journey:

- **Mash-Up Masterpieces**: Challenge DALL-E with combinations that push the boundaries of the ordinary. Think of a cactus playing the violin in Van Gogh's style. These prompts can lead to unexpected and often breathtaking results.
- **Concept Visualization**: Use DALL-E to bring abstract concepts to life. Whether it's the visual representation of "joy" or "chaos," seeing these ideas take form can be enlightening.
- **Innovative Design**: For those in design, DALL-E can be a tool for rapid prototyping. Describe your vision for a futuristic sneaker or a new kitchen gadget, and let DALL-E do the rest.

Technical Requirements

Engaging with DALL-E doesn't require being a tech wizard, but a few basic steps will smooth the way. First, ensure you have access to the platform hosting DALL-E. This might involve creating an account or signing up for a service. A stable internet connection is necessary, as DALL-E operates online, processing your prompts in the cloud.

Next, familiarize yourself with the interface. Play with different prompts to see how DALL-E responds. This exploration will help you understand the range of its capabilities and the nuances of crafting compelling descriptions.

Ethical and Copyright Considerations

The power of DALL-E brings a responsibility to navigate the ethical landscape thoughtfully. The images it generates, while novel, are based on a vast dataset of existing artwork and photographs. This raises important questions about originality and copyright:

- **Respect for Original Works**: Consider the original creators' rights implications when using DALL-E to generate images inspired by specific artists or styles. While the output is transformative, acknowledging the inspiration behind your prompts pays respect to the artists who've shaped our visual culture.
- **Usage Rights**: Review the platform's terms of service before using DALL-E images in commercial projects or publishing them online. Understanding the photos' usage rights ensures you stay within legal and ethical boundaries.
- **Ethical Creation**: Avoid prompts that could lead to harmful, offensive, or culturally insensitive content. DALL-E's beauty lies in its ability to inspire and innovate; steering clear of negative uses maintains the integrity of your creative endeavors.

DALL-E stands at the intersection of innovation and imagination. This tool democratizes art creation and opens up new avenues for visual expression. Whether you're mapping out the visuals for a story, conceptualizing a brand, or simply exploring the limits of your creativity, DALL-E is a digital muse capable of bringing the most intricate visions to life.

Unveiling Google's Gemini (formerly Bard)

In the ever-evolving landscape of technology, Google has consistently been at the forefront of innovation, pushing the boundaries of what's possible in the digital age. Among its latest ventures stands Gemini, a project shrouded in anticipation and speculation. Gemini, named after the constellation symbolizing duality and communication, represents Google's ambitious endeavor to bridge the gap between artificial intelligence (AI) and human interaction, making technology more intuitive and integrated into daily life.

Technical Foundation and Features

At its core, Gemini leverages cutting-edge AI and machine learning algorithms, standing on the shoulders of Google's extensive research and development in these areas. It's designed to understand and predict user needs with unprecedented accuracy, offering personalized assistance across various Google platforms. Critical features of Gemini include a highly adaptive AI that can learn from user interactions, a seamless integration with the Internet of Things (IoT) devices, and a revolutionary approach to data privacy, ensuring user information is protected through advanced encryption and ethical AI practices.

Impact and Applications

The implications of Gemini are far-reaching, touching every sector, from healthcare to education and beyond. In healthcare, Gemini could revolutionize patient care by providing doctors with AI-assisted diagnostics tools, while in education, it might offer personalized learning experiences tailored to each student's needs. Beyond these applications, Gemini's impact on how we interact with technology is profound, offering a glimpse into a future where technology understands us and we know it.

Challenges and Controversies

Gemini's path has its challenges. Concerns around data privacy and the ethical use of AI have sparked debates within the tech community and beyond. Google has responded by emphasizing its commitment to responsible AI development, engaging with ethical experts and policymakers to ensure Gemini adheres to the highest data protection standards and ethical AI use.

The Future of Gemini

As Gemini continues to evolve, it stands as a testament to Google's vision for the future of technology. Experts predict that Gemini will advance AI capabilities and set new standards for user interaction with digital services. Its development is closely watched by industry insiders and consumers alike, eager to see how it will shape the future of technology.

Google's Gemini represents a bold step forward in the intersection of AI and daily life. Its potential to transform industries and redefine our relationship with technology is immense, marking another milestone in Google's journey toward innovation.

AI Tools for Writers and Content Creators

The blank page is both a beginning and, sometimes, a seemingly insurmountable wall. Whether you're penning your next novel, crafting a compelling article, or concocting catchy marketing copy, the journey from the first word to the last is often fraught with hurdles. Yet, the digital age brings allies in the form of AI tools designed to assist writers and content creators in navigating the creative process with ease and flair.

AI-Assisted Writing Tools

Navigating the vast sea of ideas, sometimes writers find themselves adrift, struggling to anchor their thoughts. Here, AI-assisted writing tools come to the rescue, serving as a beacon for those lost in the fog of writer's block or the intricacies of grammar. Picture an AI companion that suggests the following line in your story and fine-tunes your prose, ensuring clarity and cohesion. These tools vary in capabilities, some focusing on generating content ideas based on a few inputs. In contrast, others specialize in enhancing grammar and style. They're like having a co-writer ready to offer a fresh perspective or a meticulous editor dedicated to polishing your sentences.

- **Idea Generation**: For those moments when inspiration is elusive, AI can suggest themes, plot twists, or even titles. It's like sparking a conversation with your muse, one prompt at a time.
- **Grammar and Style Enhancement**: Beyond the basics of spell-check, AI tools can refine your writing style, suggesting variations in sentence structure or more vivid word choices to convey your message with more significant impact.

Content Creation Platforms

The digital landscape demands content that captivates and engages audiences across various platforms. Generative AI is a powerful ally for content creators, offering platforms that streamline the workflow from ideation to publication. These platforms harness AI to assist in creating diverse content, from blog posts and social media updates to comprehensive marketing campaigns. The magic lies in their ability to understand the context and objectives of your project, generating content that aligns with your goals and resonates with your audience.

- **Versatility**: Whether your project calls for informative articles, engaging blog posts, or snappy social media content, AI platforms adapt to your needs, generating material that fits the bill.
- **Speed**: In the fast-paced world of content creation, time is of the essence. AI significantly reduces the time it takes to go from an idea to a ready-to-publish piece.

Personalization and Branding

In a world where consumers are bombarded with information, personalization isn't just excellent; it's essential. AI tools excel in tailoring content to fit not only the demographic details of your audience but also their interests and behavior patterns. This level of customization ensures that your message hits home, increasing engagement and loyalty. Moreover, maintaining a consistent brand voice across all your content is paramount. AI aids in this endeavor by learning the nuances of your brand's style and tone, ensuring that every piece of content, no matter its purpose, feels like it's from the same source.

- **Audience Insights**: AI analyzes data about your audience, offering insights that help tailor your content to their preferences and needs.
- **Brand Voice Consistency**: AI tools learn the specificities of your brand's voice and ensure that every piece of content reinforces your brand identity.

Balancing AI Assistance with Authenticity

While AI offers incredible support in the content creation process, striking a balance between leveraging this assistance and maintaining the authenticity of your voice is crucial. Authenticity connects, resonates, and builds trust with your audience, indispensable qualities in the digital age. Here's how you can achieve this balance:

- **Use AI as a Tool, Not a Crutch**: Let AI aid your creative process, not the sole creator. Use it to overcome hurdles, generate ideas, or refine your work, but ensure the final piece reflects your unique perspective and voice.
- **Edit with a Human Touch**: After using AI to draft or polish your content, go through it with a critical eye. Personalize the output further by adding personal anecdotes, emotions, or insights AI cannot replicate.
- **Stay True to Your Voice**: Regularly check that the content aligns with your voice and values when using AI tools. It's easy to get carried away with AI suggestions, but remember, the heart of your content lies in its authenticity.

AI tools are here to help, enhance, and inspire your creativity. They assist you when you're stuck and follow your lead when you're on a roll, but the unique spark of your content is always yours. As you work through your ideas, these tools make the process easier, turning your thoughts into reality.

Building Your First AI Project

Diving into your first generative AI project can feel like navigating a river at night. You know there's a path through the water, but finding it requires a bit of guidance and light. That's where this section comes in, illuminating how you craft your initial foray into AI.

Project Ideation

Dreaming up your first project starts with aligning your passions with the potential of AI. Think about what excites you; it could be anything from creating a piece of art that expresses a personal emotion to developing a tool that simplifies a daily task. Once you've pinpointed your interest, explore the AI tools that might help bring your vision to life. Remember, the goal here isn't to shoot for the moon on your first try but to pick an intriguing and achievable project.

- Think about a problem you encounter often. Is there a way AI could solve or ease it?
- Consider your hobbies. Could an AI project enhance your enjoyment or skill in one of them?

Planning and Design

Sketching a plan is your next step with your project idea. This isn't about drafting a rigid blueprint but more about setting clear, realistic goals and outlining the steps to reach them. Think about what success looks like for your project. Is it a fully functioning AI model or more about learning and exploration? From there, break down your project into smaller, manageable tasks. This approach keeps the project from overwhelming and provides a clear path forward.

- Identify the tools and resources you'll need. Do you need access to specific AI platforms or datasets?
- Set milestones. What are the critical stages of your project, and how will you know when you've reached them?

Implementation Tips

Bringing your project to life is where the real adventure begins. As you start implementing your plan, here are some practical tips to keep you on track:

- Start small. Focus on getting a basic version of your project up and running before adding complexity.
- Document your progress. Keeping a log of what works and what doesn't can be invaluable, especially when troubleshooting.
- Don't be afraid to experiment. AI projects often involve trial and error. Each misstep is a learning opportunity that brings you closer to your goal.

Finding help online is easier than you think. Online forums and communities related to your chosen AI tool are treasure troves of advice and support. Don't hesitate to ask questions or search for others who've tackled similar challenges.

Sharing and Feedback

Once you've got something to show, sharing your project with a community can be rewarding and enlightening. Whether through social media, a dedicated forum, or a presentation at a local meetup, getting feedback from others can provide fresh perspectives and ideas for improvement. Plus, discussing your project can connect you with like-minded individuals, opening doors to collaboration and new opportunities.

- Choose the right platform for sharing. Different communities have different strengths, whether technical advice, creative feedback, or moral support.
- Be open to constructive criticism. It can be challenging to hear, but it's invaluable for growth and improvement.

In wrapping up this exploration into building your first AI project, remember that every incredible journey starts with a single step. Your initial project is more than just a task; it's an entry point into a world of creativity and innovation that generative AI offers. With each project, you're expanding your skills and contributing to a broader conversation about the role of AI in shaping our future.

As we move forward, let's carry the spirit of exploration and openness that defines this chapter into the next. The journey through AI is one of continual learning and discovery, where each project, whether a soaring success or a humble learning experience, is a step toward a future where technology and creativity converge in exciting new ways.

EIGHT

The AI Learning Curve: Resources to Get You Going

Picture a kid standing in front of a massive library. She's got that wide-eyed look, not just because of the sheer volume of books but because each one holds the key to a new world, a piece of the puzzle in understanding something vast. That's you right now, in the digital age, ready to unlock the secrets of generative AI. But where do you begin in this enormous library of information and tools at your disposal? This chapter is your map, pointing you to the resources that will turn the lock.

Online Courses and Resources for AI Learning

The internet is overflowing with courses on AI, but not all are created equal. Sorting through them can feel like trying to find a whisper in a thunderstorm. Here's how to find the ones that will add to the noise and honestly guide you through learning AI.

Comprehensive Learning Platforms

Start with platforms known for their depth and quality. Coursera, edX, and Udacity stand out for their partnerships with top universities and tech companies, offering courses that range from beginner to advanced levels. These platforms often provide free and paid content, with opportunities to earn certificates that can beef up your resume. For instance, Coursera's "AI For Everyone" by Andrew Ng gives a solid foundation without assuming prior knowledge. At the same time, Udacity's Nanodegree programs are project-based, offering hands-on experience.

- **Tip**: Look for courses with high ratings and reviews that mention hands-on projects and clear explanations. This can help ensure the course matches your learning style and goals.

Specialized Workshops and Webinars

Sometimes, diving deep into a specific topic under expert guidance can illuminate aspects of AI you'd never considered. Many industry leaders and educational institutions host workshops and webinars, offering a deeper dive into specialized areas of AI. For example, the NVIDIA Deep Learning Institute provides workshops on AI applications in fields from healthcare to game development.

- **Tip**: Check the event pages of major tech companies or universities and sign up for newsletters in your areas of interest. This way, you won't miss registration periods for these valuable sessions.

Free Resources

A wealth of free resources is available for those just dipping their toes in or operating on a tight budget. Websites like Fast.ai offer practical, coder-friendly courses designed to get you up and running with deep learning. At the same time, MIT's

OpenCourseWare makes lecture notes, exams, and videos from its AI courses available to all.

- **Visual Element**: A curated list infographic detailing the top free AI learning resources, including direct links and a brief description of what each offers.

Staying Updated

With AI evolving at breakneck speed, staying in the loop is crucial. Subscribing to newsletters like O'Reilly's AI newsletter, following thought leaders on social media, or joining AI-focused news sites like The Algorithm by MIT Technology Review can inform you about the latest developments, tools, and insights.

- **Interactive Element**: A quiz titled "Which AI Resource Fits Your Learning Style?" helps you identify the type of AI learning resource that might suit you best based on your preferences and goals.

Where to Start?

With so many options, the question remains: where to begin? Start by setting clear, achievable goals. Are you looking to understand AI concepts for your current job, or are you aiming to switch careers? Maybe you're just curious. Your goal will determine which resources will be most beneficial. From there, dedicate a set amount of weekly time to your AI education. Consistency beats cramming when it comes to truly understanding and retaining new information.

Remember, every expert in AI once stood where you are now, at the beginning of their learning path. The resources outlined here are your first steps on your unique path. Whether you're looking to transform your career or expand your knowledge, AI learning is rich with opportunities to grow and explore.

Community and Forum Engagement for AI Enthusiasts

You don't have to explore AI alone. There are communities and forums online and in cities worldwide filled with enthusiasts, professionals, and newcomers all passionate about AI. These places are vibrant with ideas, debates, and collaborations, offering much more than just information.

Finding Your Community

The first step in this adventure is discovering where your tribe congregates. Online forums such as Reddit's r/MachineLearning or Stack Overflow offer a broad spectrum of discussions ranging from beginner questions to deep theoretical debates. Suppose your interests are more specific, such as ethical AI, neural networks, or AI in healthcare. In that case, niche communities exist for almost every sub-field. LinkedIn groups and Twitter hashtags can lead you to these specialized forums. Remember, the goal is to find a space that answers your questions, challenges your understanding, and grows with you as you delve deeper into AI.

- Start by identifying your AI interests or the questions you seek answers to.
- Use search engines with specific keywords related to your AI interests to find relevant online communities and forums.
- Explore the content and vibe of a community before diving in. The space must align with your learning style and values.

Benefits of Community Engagement

Once you've found your community, the real magic begins. Engagement in these forums comes with a treasure trove of benefits. You often gain access to the latest AI resources, tools, and news before they hit the mainstream. Networking opportunities abound, connecting you with mentors, collaborators, or potential employers. Through active participation, you can exchange knowledge and receive insights and advice that could propel your projects and understanding forward. Moreover, these communities offer a sense of belonging, a reminder that you're part of a global movement shaping the future.

- The exchange of knowledge and resources keeps you updated and accelerates your learning.
- Networking opportunities open doors to mentorship, collaboration, and career advancements.
- A sense of belonging fosters motivation and encouragement during challenging learning phases.

Participating in Discussions

Diving into discussions might seem daunting initially, but your voice and perspective are invaluable. Start by lurking, getting a feel for the community's norms and the types of discussions. When you're ready, begin by responding to others' posts. Offer your insights, ask clarifying questions, or share resources. As you become more comfortable, initiate your discussions. Remember, every expert in the forum once posted their first comment, too. Your questions and contributions add value, sparking discussions that could lead to new insights for you and others.

- Lurk first to understand the community norms and discussion styles.

- Begin responding to others' posts to integrate yourself into the community gradually.
- Don't hesitate to start discussions. Your perspective could be the catalyst for fascinating exchanges.

Local Meetups and Conferences

While online forums offer convenience and a broad network, there's something irreplaceable about face-to-face interactions. Local meetups, workshops, and conferences provide these opportunities, allowing you to meet fellow AI enthusiasts in your area. These gatherings can range from informal coffee meetups discussing the latest AI news to more structured workshops where you can get hands-on experience with AI tools. Conversely, conferences offer a larger stage, showcasing cutting-edge research, panel discussions, and networking events with leaders in the field.

- Use platforms like Meetup.com to find AI groups in your locality.
- Check out university bulletin boards or websites for workshops and guest lectures open to the public.
- Attend conferences not just for the sessions but for the coffee breaks and evening mixers where you can mingle and connect.

Engaging with AI communities and forums is like adding a turbocharger to your learning journey. Through these interactions, you expand your knowledge and build a network of contacts who can support and inspire you as you grow. Whether finding the answer to a perplexing problem, discovering a new tool that revolutionizes your workflow, or connecting to a collaborative project, the value of community engagement in AI cannot be overstated. Remember, in the vast, ever-evolving landscape of AI, you're not alone. Communities and forums are your compass, guiding you through and offering support, insight, and companionship along the way.

Challenges and Competitions to Sharpen Your AI Skills

While exhilarating, diving into the world of AI can sometimes feel like navigating a vast ocean in a small boat. Imagine discovering a compass that points north and nudges your boat faster toward your destination. That's what AI challenges and competitions offer—a beacon to guide and accelerate your journey in the AI landscape. These platforms are not just about winning; they're about expanding your horizon, testing your skills against real-world problems, and connecting with a community that shares your passion.

AI Challenges and Competitions

Across the digital landscape, numerous platforms host AI challenges and competitions, each tailored to different skill levels and interests. Websites like Kaggle, DrivenData, and CodaLab serve as arenas where enthusiasts, from beginners to seasoned professionals, can engage in tasks ranging from predictive modeling to creating algorithms that can artfully dodge obstacles in video games. These contests range broadly in scope and theme, covering everything from data science to generative art, reflecting the diverse applications of AI in solving both practical and abstract challenges.

- Starting with smaller, less intimidating competitions can help build confidence for those new to AI.
- Exploring competitions that align with your interests or professional aspirations can make the experience more engaging and rewarding.

Learning through Competition

Participating in these competitions does more than just put your skills to the test; it propels your learning forward at an impressive pace. Facing real-world problems, you're compelled to apply theory in practical scenarios, pushing you to explore new techniques, tools, and methodologies. The iterative process of hypothesizing, testing, and refining your models in response to competition feedback is a potent learning experience, often more impactful than traditional classroom scenarios.

- Engaging with a problem without a clear-cut answer encourages creative thinking and innovation.
- The competitive aspect adds motivation, pushing you to learn and apply new concepts or techniques you might have overlooked.

Team Collaboration

One of the most enriching aspects of these competitions is the opportunity for team collaboration. Joining forces with others allows you to pool diverse skills, knowledge, and perspectives, often leading to more innovative solutions than any individual could have developed alone. Collaboration in this context isn't just about dividing tasks; it's a dynamic process of learning from one another, challenging each other's ideas, and collectively pushing toward a common goal.

- Teams can leverage members' strengths while compensating for individual weaknesses, creating a more resilient problem-solving unit.
- Collaborating with a global team exposes you to different approaches and problem-solving techniques, broadening your understanding of AI.

Recognition and Opportunities

Excelling in AI competitions can open doors to recognition and opportunities that extend far beyond the satisfaction of solving complex problems. Winners and top performers often attract attention from industry leaders, research institutions, and tech companies. This leads to job offers, invitations to speak at conferences, or collaboration opportunities on research projects. Even for those who don't clinch the top spots, the experience gained, and the connections made during these competitions can be invaluable, enhancing your resume and expanding your professional network.

- Many competitions offer cash prizes, internships, or scholarships to winners, providing tangible rewards for your efforts.
- Participating in competitions demonstrates a proactive approach to learning and problem-solving, traits highly valued in the tech industry.

As you navigate the exciting world of AI, remember that challenges and competitions are more than just contests; they're catalysts for growth, learning, and connection. Whether you're coding late into the night to meet a competition deadline, brainstorming with teammates from across the globe, or presenting your innovative solution to a panel of experts, you're not just building AI models; you're building a future where your skills, knowledge, and creativity play a pivotal role in shaping the landscape of technology and society.

The Importance of a Growth Mindset in AI Learning

Becoming skilled in AI requires patience, the right tools, enduring challenges, and a constant commitment to growth. In this dynamic field, adopting a growth mindset isn't just helpful; it's crucial. This mindset allows your skills and knowledge to flourish, transforming challenges into opportunities for development.

Embracing Challenges

When diving into AI, expect to meet challenges head-on. These aren't just hurdles; they're opportunities disguised in tough wrapping. Every error message, every failed model, and every confusing dataset invites you to engage more deeply with the problem at hand. These challenges make concepts more straightforward, sharpen your skills, and deepen your understanding.

- When a project doesn't go as planned, step back and analyze what went wrong and why. This reflection turns a moment of failure into a valuable learning experience.
- Push your boundaries by taking on projects slightly outside your comfort zone. The discomfort you feel is the stretching of your capabilities.

Continuous Learning

In the ever-shifting landscape of AI, the only constant is change. New algorithms, tools, and applications emerge at breakneck speed, making continuous learning an advantage and a necessity. Keeping up with the latest advancements ensures your skills remain relevant and sharp. But more than that, it feeds your curiosity and passion for the field, keeping the flame of excitement alive.

- Dedicate time each week to learning something new, whether it's a recent paper, a tool update, or a concept you still need to explore.
- Mix up your learning sources. Combine online courses with podcasts, blogs, and research papers to engage with content from multiple angles.

Seeking Feedback

Feedback is your compass in the journey of AI mastery. It points you in the right direction, highlighting areas of strength and those needing improvement. Engage with peers, mentors, and AI communities to share your work and seek their insights. Their perspectives can offer new angles and ideas you might have yet to consider, pushing your projects from good to great.

- Be proactive in asking for feedback. After presenting your work, ask specific questions to guide the kind of feedback you're looking for.
- Approach feedback with an open mind. Constructive criticism is a gift that can drive your growth, even if it's tough to hear at times.

Celebrating Milestones

Every step forward on your AI learning path deserves recognition. Regardless of size, celebrating milestones reinforces your progress and motivates you to keep moving forward. Did you finally understand a concept that baffled you for weeks? Or perhaps you've completed a project you've been working on for months. These achievements are markers of your growth and commitment to learning AI.

- Keep a "win" journal. Note down every success, big or small. Reviewing this journal can boost your morale during challenging times.
- Share your achievements with your community. This will allow you to celebrate with those who've supported you and inspire others on their learning paths.

In developing your AI skills, having a growth mindset helps you see obstacles as opportunities. It's a perspective that encourages resilience, fosters continuous learning, values feedback, and celebrates each step forward. This mindset isn't just about developing technical prowess; it's about cultivating an approach to learning and problem-solving that benefits every area of your life. As you navigate the complexities of AI, remember that growth is a process, not a destination. Each challenge encountered, lesson learned, and milestone achieved is a step toward mastering AI and evolving as a lifelong learner and innovator in this fascinating field.

Future-Proofing Your Career with AI Skills

In a world where the only constant is change, aligning your career trajectory with the advancements in AI isn't just a wise move—it's practically a necessity. The demand for AI skills spans across industries, making it clear that these capabilities will be a significant part of the professional landscape.

AI Skills in Demand

Right now, industries from healthcare to finance and beyond are looking for professionals who can interpret and implement AI technologies. Skills such as machine learning, natural language processing, robotics, and AI ethics are sought after and rewarded with career growth and stability. The versatility of AI applications means that understanding these technologies can propel careers in unexpected and exciting directions.

- Data analysis and interpretation are foundational to AI, making them invaluable skills.
- Programming knowledge, especially in languages like Python, is often a prerequisite for more advanced AI work.
- Integrating and applying AI solutions to real-world problems is an increasingly important skill set across various fields.

Integrating AI into Your Career

No matter your current role, there's a path to incorporating AI skills to elevate your position or open new doors. For those in marketing, mastering AI tools for data analysis can provide insights into consumer behavior. Educators can leverage AI to create personalized learning experiences. Even artists find a new medium for expression and creation in AI. The key is identifying how AI technologies intersect with your field and pursuing the knowledge and skills that will enable you to bring these innovative solutions to your work.

- Start with an audit of how AI is used in your field and where it's headed.
- Identify skills or tools aligning with your career goals and build expertise.

Lifelong Learning Plans

Staying relevant in the AI era requires an ongoing commitment to learning. Crafting a lifelong learning plan helps you stay on top of AI trends and ensures your skills evolve as fast as the technologies.

This plan might include yearly goals, such as completing specific courses, attending workshops, earning certifications, and daily or weekly habits, like reading AI research papers or building small projects to test new skills.

- Set achievable goals that push your understanding and application of AI forward.
- Formal education, such as online courses and certifications, and informal learning activities, like project-based learning or community discussions.

Networking and Professional Development

Building a network with other AI enthusiasts and professionals can provide support, inspiration, and opportunities. Professional development activities, such as attending conferences, joining AI-focused organizations, or even volunteering on AI projects, can increase your visibility in the field and connect you with people who can help advance your career. Online platforms offer a great way to start networking, but consider the value of face-to-face interactions in building meaningful connections.

- Participate in AI forums and discussions to showcase your knowledge and learn from others.
- Attend industry events and try to engage with speakers and attendees. These connections can be invaluable sources of information and opportunities.

By focusing on the AI skills in demand, integrating AI into your current career path, committing to lifelong learning, and engaging in networking and professional development, you're not just future-proofing your career but setting yourself up as a valuable player in a world where AI is ubiquitous.

With every industry looking to AI for solutions, the potential for growth and innovation is immense. Whether you're just starting or looking to pivot your career, the AI revolution offers a landscape ripe with opportunities for those willing to invest in their skills and engage with the community.

As we finish exploring the AI skills landscape and how to incorporate them into your career, remember that the future is shaped by the skills we learn, the connections we make, and the challenges we take on. The next chapter is waiting, with more insights and strategies to help you navigate this exciting digital era.

NINE

The Frontier of Generative AI: Today's Research, Tomorrow's Reality

Imagine flipping through the pages of a science fiction novel, where the boundaries between the imaginable and the achievable blur. Now, picture this not as a dive into fiction but as a peek into the laboratories and minds shaping the future of generative AI. This chapter isn't just about what's happening; it's about the ripple effect of today's research on our tomorrow.

Pioneering Techniques

Generative AI, a field once shackled by data and computing power limitations, is witnessing a renaissance. The latest research isn't just pushing the envelope; it's redesigning it entirely. For instance, few-shot and transfer learning teach AI systems to understand and create with significantly less data than previously thought possible. Imagine teaching a child to draw a cat by showing them just one picture instead of a hundred. That's the kind of efficiency leap we're talking about.

- **Few-Shot Learning**: This technique enables AI to

perform tasks accurately with minimal data, breaking the data-hungry stereotype of machine learning.
- **Transfer Learning**: Here, a model developed for one task is repurposed for a second related task. It's like learning to play the ukulele when you already know the guitar; you're not starting from scratch.

Impact on Efficiency

The impact of these innovations extends beyond academic curiosity. They're making AI more scalable, accessible, and environmentally friendly. Scalable because less data means AI can be trained faster and cheaper. Accessible because it lowers the barrier to entry for individuals and small teams without the resources of tech giants. Environmentally friendly because less computing power reduces energy consumption. It's a win-win-win scenario.

For example, training a single AI model can require as much electricity as a small town uses in a month. Researchers directly contribute to a more sustainable AI future by making models more data-efficient.

Interdisciplinary Approaches

The most groundbreaking AI research often happens at the crossroads of disciplines. When computer scientists meet with linguists, artists, or ethicists, they fuse their expertise to solve complex problems in novel ways. This interdisciplinary approach is breeding a new generation of more intelligent AI systems that are more attuned to human needs and ethics.

Take, for instance, the collaboration between AI researchers and psychologists to understand and generate human-like emotions in AI. This synergy paves the way for AI systems that can provide more nuanced and empathetic interactions, whether in customer service bots or mental health apps.

- **AI and Linguistics**: By combining these fields, researchers develop models that understand and generate human language with unprecedented accuracy and subtlety.
- **AI and Art**: Artists and AI researchers collaborate to create generative art that challenges our understanding of creativity and authorship.

Future Possibilities

Speculating about the future based on current research is like trying to read tea leaves, but some trends are clear. Generative AI is moving toward a future where interaction with AI will be indistinguishable from human interaction in terms of complexity and empathy. Moreover, democratizing AI tools means that AI creation won't require a Ph.D. in computer science soon. It'll be as accessible as using a smartphone.

- **Indistinguishable Interactions**: With advancements in language models and emotional AI, future AI systems could provide companionship and support that feels genuinely human.
- **Democratization of AI Tools**: As AI becomes more user-friendly, we'll see an explosion of creativity and innovation from all corners of society. The impact will be ubiquitous, from teenagers in their bedrooms creating viral content to small businesses revolutionizing their operations.

Visual Element: Infographic on "The Evolution of Generative AI." An infographic showcasing a timeline of key milestones in generative AI research, from the inception of neural networks to the latest breakthroughs in efficiency and interdisciplinary approaches. Each milestone is accompanied by a brief explanation of its impact on the field.

Interactive Element: Quiz "Which AI Innovation Will Shape Your Future?" This short, engaging quiz prompts readers to answer questions about their interests and challenges. Based on their responses, the quiz suggests which AI research areas might most impact their personal or professional lives, encouraging further exploration and learning.

In sum, while today's research in generative AI might seem like the stuff of science fiction, it's rapidly shaping a reality where the full potential of human creativity can be unleashed, supported by machines that learn, adapt, and create alongside us. The ripple effect of these innovations promises a future where AI is not a tool of the few but a collaborator for the many, transforming how we live, work, and express ourselves creatively.

AI in Space Exploration and Environmental Science

Space, the final frontier, and our planet, the cradle of life, are arenas where AI plays an increasingly pivotal role. From the vast emptiness of space to the complex web of ecosystems on Earth, AI is not just a participant but a leading force in exploration, analysis, and conservation efforts.

Space Exploration

With their high stakes and remote operations, space missions benefit significantly from generative AI's predictive capabilities and its power to simulate complex scenarios. AI models are complicated at work before a spacecraft leaves the drawing board, simulating countless mission scenarios. These simulations, ranging from orbital mechanics to life support systems, help engineers and scientists foresee potential issues and fine-tune designs to withstand the harsh conditions of space.

- AI's role extends to analyzing data from space probes. As probes venture further into space and send back petabytes of data, AI helps sift through this information, identifying points of interest that might elude human observers. For instance, AI algorithms have identified new craters on Mars and potential signs of water or volcanic activity on distant moons, data crucial for planning future missions and understanding our solar system.
- AI is also training to take on more autonomous roles in spacecraft operations. It learns to navigate, make decisions, and even perform repairs—crucial skills for missions to Mars and beyond, where real-time human intervention isn't feasible due to the vast distances involved.

Environmental Monitoring

Back on Earth, AI is turning its gaze toward our environment, offering tools to monitor ecosystems with unprecedented detail. Satellite imagery analyzed with AI provides insights into changes in forest cover, urban expansion, and the health of our oceans. What makes AI indispensable in this field is its ability not just to capture snapshots of the current state but to track changes over time, revealing trends that guide conservation efforts.

- AI models can now predict environmental changes, from ice caps melting to endangered species migration patterns. This predictive power is essential for planning conservation strategies, allowing us to act before it's too late.

Climate Change

AI's potential shines brightest in the fight against climate change. AI is at the forefront of climate change research, offering models that predict future climate scenarios with increasing accuracy. These models consider countless variables, from atmospheric CO_2 levels to ocean temperatures, helping scientists understand potential future climates and the impacts of various mitigation strategies.

- Beyond prediction, AI is optimizing solutions to combat climate change. One exciting area is carbon capture technology. AI algorithms optimize extracting CO_2 from the atmosphere, making it more efficient and cost-effective. Similarly, AI optimizes energy consumption in buildings and industrial processes, reducing greenhouse gas emissions and helping industries transition to greener operations.

Sustainable Solutions

The quest for sustainability drives innovation, with AI leading the way in creating solutions to some of our most pressing environmental challenges. From intelligent agriculture practices that minimize water use and maximize yield to AI-driven platforms that streamline recycling processes, AI is making sustainability an ideal and practical reality.

- In agriculture, AI systems analyze data from drones, satellites, and ground sensors to monitor crop health, predict yields, and provide farmers with actionable insights. This data-driven approach ensures resources are used efficiently, reducing waste and environmental impact.
- AI has also revolutionized waste management. Innovative sorting systems can accurately separate recyclable materials, increasing the efficiency of recycling processes and reducing the amount of waste sent to landfills.
- On the energy front, AI is optimizing renewable energy production. By predicting wind patterns and sunlight exposure, AI helps manage wind farms and solar panels, maximizing output and making renewable energy sources more reliable and efficient.

In both the boundless reaches of space and the intricate ecosystems of Earth, AI stands as a beacon of progress. It navigates spacecraft through the cosmos, deciphers the secrets hidden in vast data streams, and crafts strategies to preserve our planet. The application of AI in these fields is not just about technological advancement; it's a testament to our enduring quest to explore, understand, and protect the only home we've ever known and the vast universe that surrounds it.

The Next Frontier: AI in Quantum Computing

Quantum computing is about to revolutionize how we process information. Combined with AI, it will take us into areas we once thought were only possible in science fiction. Integrating quantum computing with AI marks a leap toward tackling computational challenges that traditional computers grapple with, opening doors to unprecedented advancements.

Quantum Computing Explained

At its core, quantum computing departs from classical computing through its foundational principles, which are hinged on the laws of quantum mechanics. Unlike classical bits, which process tasks in a binary state of 0s or 1s, quantum computing operates with qubits. Thanks to a phenomenon known as superposition, these qubits can exist in a state of 0, 1, or both simultaneously. This ability allows quantum computers to process complex, large-scale computations more efficiently than their classical counterparts.

- Superposition and entanglement are other quantum phenomena in which qubits become interdependent. This enables instant communication regardless of distance, giving quantum computers their edge. This leap in processing capability holds profound implications for AI, potentially speeding up data analysis and model training processes exponentially.

Enhancing AI Capabilities

The fusion of quantum computing and AI promises to supercharge AI's data analysis and pattern recognition faculties. By leveraging quantum computers' parallel processing abilities, AI can sift through vast datasets more swiftly and accurately, identifying patterns and correlations that would take conventional computers much longer to uncover.

- This synergy could significantly enhance AI models used in drug discovery, allowing researchers to analyze molecular structures and interactions at a pace

unimaginable with current technology. Similarly, quantum-enhanced AI could revolutionize risk assessment models in finance by analyzing market data across multiple variables and scenarios in real time.
- Furthermore, quantum computing could break new ground in machine learning, particularly optimization problems. The ability to evaluate multiple solutions simultaneously could lead to more efficient and effective algorithms, honing AI's decision-making and problem-solving capabilities.

Challenges and Opportunities

While integrating AI with quantum computing has great potential, it also presents challenges. The nascent nature of quantum technology means that stability, error rates, and qubit coherence times must be overcome. Developing algorithms fully utilizing quantum computing's capabilities is also in its infancy.

- Another significant challenge lies in the quantum hardware itself. Building a quantum computer capable of outperforming classical supercomputers for practical tasks—a milestone known as quantum supremacy—requires maintaining qubits in a coherent quantum state for extended periods, a feat that's currently technologically demanding.
- Despite these challenges, the opportunities are vast. Quantum computing could enable AI to tackle intractable problems today, such as simulating complex biological processes or optimizing large-scale logistical operations. Moreover, the potential for quantum encryption promises to revolutionize data security, offering a safeguard against the

vulnerabilities of current encryption methods to quantum attacks.

Timeline for Integration

It is very uncertain to predict when quantum computing and AI will fully integrate and reach their potential. However, there are promising signs. Research labs and tech companies have already achieved quantum supremacy for specific tasks, a step toward broader applications.

- In the near term, we may see hybrid models where quantum and classical computing work together, with quantum processors handling specific tasks within more extensive AI algorithms run on classical computers.
- Most estimates range from a decade to several decades away for widespread, practical applications of AI powered by quantum computing. This timeline will depend on quantum hardware, algorithm development breakthroughs, and concerted efforts to surmount the existing technical challenges.

The prospect of AI-enhanced quantum computing invites us to reconsider the limits of what's computationally possible. As researchers untangle the complexities of quantum mechanics and refine the algorithms that will drive this next technological epoch, we stand on the cusp of a future where AI's capacity to learn, analyze, and create is unfettered by the constraints of classical computing. This horizon, where quantum computing and AI converge, heralds a new era of innovation with the potential to redefine industries, accelerate scientific discovery, and transform our understanding of the world.

Ethical AI: Toward More Responsible Innovations

In the blossoming garden of AI, the seeds of ethical AI are sown with the hope that they will mature into technologies that advance our capabilities, and they do so with a moral compass in hand. Ethical AI isn't an abstract concept; it's the backbone of ensuring that AI innovations uplift humanity, safeguard rights, and promote fairness.

What Makes AI Ethical?

Ethical AI revolves around creating and deploying AI systems that respect human values and rights. It's about programming not just for efficiency and capability but with a keen eye on the consequences of these technologies. AI must not only aim not to harm but actively contribute to the well-being of individuals and society. This includes ensuring privacy, enhancing equity, and promoting inclusivity.

- Ethical AI demands transparency, clarifying how AI systems make decisions. This is crucial for trust, especially in applications like healthcare or justice, where lives and liberties are at stake.
- Moreover, AI must be accountable. When AI systems impact people's lives, it's vital to have mechanisms to answer for good or bad outcomes.
- Lastly, ethical AI champions fairness. It works against bias, treating all individuals and groups equally and fairly.

Frameworks and Guidelines

Various frameworks and guidelines are compasses in navigating the path to ethical AI. For instance, the European Commission's

AI Ethics Guidelines list seven critical requirements for trustworthy AI: human agency, technical robustness, and privacy. Similarly, the IEEE's Ethically Aligned Design provides comprehensive principles for prioritizing human well-being in AI systems.

- These frameworks serve as foundations for organizations to build their ethical AI strategies. They provide a starting point for considering the wide-ranging impacts of AI technologies.
- Adopting these guidelines helps organizations avoid ethical pitfalls and innovate in ways that respect and enhance human dignity.

Role of AI Ethics Boards

With the stakes so high, the role of ethics boards in guiding AI research and applications has never been more critical. These boards, comprised of experts from diverse fields such as technology, philosophy, law, and social sciences, review AI projects to ensure they align with ethical standards and societal values.

- Ethics boards do more than greenlight projects. They provide ongoing advice, helping teams navigate complex ethical landscapes and adjust their trajectories as needed.
- Their impact extends to outside organizations, too. They contribute to the broader ethical AI dialogue by publishing their findings and recommendations and setting industry benchmarks.

Overcoming Challenges in Enforcement

The road to ethical AI is fraught with technical and philosophical obstacles. They enforce ethical guidelines in a field as fast-paced and decentralized as AI presents a unique set of challenges.

- One such challenge is the global nature of AI development. Finding common ground is daunting with researchers and companies across countries with varying legal and ethical standards.
- Another hurdle is the complexity of AI systems themselves. As AI advances, understanding and predicting its behavior becomes more complex, challenging adherence to ethical guidelines.
- There's also the issue of economic pressure. In the race to innovate, companies might overlook ethical considerations in favor of speed and profitability.

A multifaceted approach is necessary to navigate these challenges:

- **Global Cooperation**: By fostering international dialogue and cooperation, we can work toward universal standards for ethical AI. This includes agreements on privacy, data use, and fairness that transcend borders.
- **Technical Solutions**: Innovations in AI transparency and explainability can help demystify AI decisions, making it easier to align with ethical guidelines. Techniques like "AI auditing" could become standard practice, assessing AI systems for ethical compliance before deployment.
- **Ethical Leadershi**p: Companies and institutions can lead by example, prioritizing ethical considerations in their AI projects and encouraging a culture where ethical AI is celebrated and rewarded. This includes investing in ethical AI research and development to solve the most pressing challenges.

- **Public Engagement**: Empowering the public with knowledge about AI and its impacts ensures a broader scrutiny base and support for ethical AI. This includes education initiatives and public forums for discussing AI ethics.

Ethical considerations must be at the forefront of innovation in cultivating a future where AI serves as a force for good. This journey requires vigilance, collaboration, and a steadfast commitment to the values that define us as a society. Through frameworks, ethics boards, and concerted efforts to overcome enforcement challenges, we pave the way for AI technologies that push the boundaries of what's possible and do so with integrity and respect for human dignity.

Predicting the Unpredictable: AI's Role in Future Predictions

In modern technology, generative AI has become a key part of making predictions, giving us insights into future possibilities. From weather patterns to market shifts, AI's predictive prowess is reshaping our anticipation of what's to come, turning the once murky waters of the future into more apparent streams of possibility.

Advanced Predictive Models

Generative AI is at the forefront of creating models that forecast outcomes across diverse domains with increasing sophistication. In healthcare, AI predicts disease outbreaks by analyzing patterns in data streams that human experts might overlook. Financial analysts rely on AI to anticipate market fluctuations, allowing for strategic adjustments before changes take hold. Even in public safety, AI systems forecast potential disaster zones, enabling preemptive measures that save lives and resources.

- In agriculture, AI's predictions on crop yields help farmers make informed decisions, optimize harvests, and reduce waste.
- Urban planning benefits from AI's ability to simulate population growth and movement, aiding in designing more sustainable cities.

Accuracy and Reliability

Triumphs and trials mark the journey toward reliable AI-driven predictions. Achieving high accuracy remains a challenge, as the complexities of the natural world often defy even the most sophisticated models. Yet, strides in machine learning algorithms and data processing have significantly improved AI's predictive accuracy. Continuous learning models adapt to new data, refining their forecasts over time while integrating diverse data sources to offer a more rounded view of potential futures.

- The variance in data quality and quantity directly impacts predictive accuracy. As such, efforts to standardize and cleanse data before it feeds into AI models are crucial.
- The transparency of AI predictions also plays a role in their reliability. When users understand how AI reaches its conclusions, they can better interpret and trust its forecasts.

Impact on Decision-Making

The ripple effects of AI's predictive capabilities touch every decision-making corner. In business, leaders use AI to forecast trends, guiding strategies that keep them ahead of the curve. Governments employ AI to anticipate social and economic shifts, crafting policies that address future needs. Even individuals benefit, as AI offers personalized predictions that inform everything from health decisions to financial planning.

- AI-driven predictions enable more proactive approaches in almost every sector, reducing reactive measures that often come with higher costs and risks.
- The democratization of predictive AI tools means that access to future insights is no longer confined to organizations with vast resources.

Ethical Considerations

With great power comes great responsibility, and the ethical implications of relying on AI for predictions necessitate careful consideration. Ensuring that AI models do not perpetuate biases or inequalities is paramount. Data privacy must be safeguarded, as the personal information used to fuel predictions carries the risk of misuse in the wrong hands. Additionally, the accountability for decisions based on AI predictions must be clearly defined, balancing leveraging AI's insights and retaining human oversight.

- The potential for AI to influence public opinion and behavior through predictions, especially in areas like elections or public health, underscores the need for ethical transparency.
- Establishing guidelines for the responsible use of predictive AI, including audits for bias and mechanisms for data protection, is critical to fostering trust and ensuring that predictions serve the common good.

The blend of excitement and caution is palpable as we stand on the precipice of a world increasingly informed by AI-driven forecasts. The advancements in predictive models open doors to understanding and preparing for futures that were once beyond our grasp. Yet, the journey toward harnessing this potential responsibly is ongoing, framed by the dual goals of innovation and ethical integrity.

Looking ahead, the dialogue on predictive AI continues to evolve, reflecting a broader conversation about the role of technology in shaping our world. As we move into the next chapter, the exploration deepens, touching on how AI forecasts the future and actively shapes it through creative and constructive applications. The promise of AI extends beyond seeing what's to come; it lies in our ability to use these insights to build a future that reflects our highest aspirations for society.

TEN

Riding the Wave: Adapting to AI's Evolution

Picture this: a surfer spots a towering wave in the distance. Instead of paddling away as it nears, they adjust their stance, ready to ride it. That's a lot like facing the advancements in AI. Rather than being overwhelmed or dodging the changes, there's a knack for adjusting our skills and mindset to ride the wave and enjoy the journey it takes us on. This chapter is about making those adjustments, ensuring you're equipped and ready to navigate the evolving landscape of AI.

Essential AI Skills

Certain AI and machine learning skills stand out in the growing market of future job opportunities. Skills in data analysis and interpretation are essential for almost any AI task. Proficiency in programming languages, especially Python, is crucial for developing and understanding AI algorithms. Knowledge of machine learning techniques and neural networks is important for navigating AI's complexities. Don't forget soft skills like critical thinking, problem-solving, and effective communication—key to succeeding in this field.

- Data Analysis and Interpretation
- Programming (Python, R)
- Machine Learning and Neural Networks
- Critical Thinking and Problem-Solving

Lifelong Learning

Adopting a lifelong learning approach in the context of AI is like treating every wave as an opportunity to improve your surfing skills. The AI field evolves rapidly, with discoveries and technologies emerging constantly. Staying updated means you're always ready for the next big wave. Set aside time each week to learn something new, whether it's through online courses, webinars, or podcasts. Join AI forums or local meetups to exchange knowledge with peers. And remember, learning from mistakes is part of the process. Every wipeout has a lesson that prepares you for your next ride.

- Regularly update your skills through courses and webinars.
- Engage with AI communities for knowledge exchange.
- Learn from mistakes and stay curious.

Interdisciplinary Knowledge

The future of AI doesn't exist in a vacuum. It intersects with various fields, from healthcare and finance to art and environmental science. Imagine if a surfer only knew how to ride one type of wave. They'd miss out when conditions change. Similarly, understanding AI's application across different domains enriches your perspective and opens up many opportunities. For instance, knowledge about AI's role in diagnosing diseases could be revolutionary if you're in healthcare. AI might become your next medium or muse if you're an artist. Dive into journals, attend interdisciplinary conferences, and collaborate on projects outside your comfort zone to broaden your understanding and application of AI.

- Explore AI applications in your field of interest.
- Collaborate on interdisciplinary projects.
- Broaden your knowledge through diverse resources.

Preparing the Workforce

As the AI wave reshapes the landscape, the workforce must adapt. Companies and educational institutions play a crucial role in this transition. Offering training programs and workshops can update employees' and students' skills, making them proficient in AI tools and applications relevant to their field. Schools and universities should integrate AI and machine learning into their curriculums in computer science departments and across all disciplines. Moreover, fostering an environment that encourages experimentation with AI is crucial, even if it means facing failures. Think of it as teaching someone to surf; they need to understand the waves, but getting on the board and facing the waves themselves is where the real learning happens.

- Implement AI training programs in workplaces.
- Integrate AI education across all academic disciplines.
- Encourage hands-on experimentation with AI.

Visual Element: AI Skills Infographic

This vibrant infographic maps out the "AI Skills Landscape," highlighting critical skills needed to thrive in an AI-driven future. It breaks down technical skills like programming and machine learning alongside soft skills such as problem-solving and adaptability. Each skill is accompanied by tips on developing it and its relevance in various industries.

Interactive Element: AI Readiness Quiz

This is a fun and engaging quiz titled "How AI-Ready Are You?" Participants answer questions about their current skills, learning habits, and openness to interdisciplinary learning. Based on their responses, they receive personalized advice on areas to focus on, resources to explore, and the following steps to take on their AI learning journey.

By embracing the essential AI skills, committing to lifelong learning, exploring interdisciplinary knowledge, and actively preparing the workforce, you're not just ready to ride the AI wave; you're set to make the most of it. The future is an exciting blend of challenges and opportunities, and with the right mindset and skills, you're well-equipped to thrive in an AI-enhanced world.

The Role of Education in an AI-Enhanced World

In a world progressively intertwined with AI, the educational landscape must evolve to meet the demands of tomorrow. This evolution isn't just about adding a few coding or machine learning courses. It's about rethinking our approach to learning and teaching and the resources we provide to fuel curiosity and innovation in AI.

Curriculum Changes

The first step is updating the curriculum to include AI literacy from a young age. This doesn't mean every first-grader needs to start coding, but introducing AI concepts and how they impact our daily lives can demystify the technology and spark interest. For example, storytelling around how AI helps predict weather can make the subject relatable. As students grow, these stories can evolve into more complex discussions on AI's role in various sectors, laying a solid foundation for advanced learning in later years. This gradual buildup ensures that by the time students make career choices, they're well-informed about AI's possibilities.

- Starting with simple, relatable examples of AI in everyday life.
- Gradually increasing the complexity of AI concepts as students advance.
- Ensuring AI literacy is part of the foundational education for all students.

Teacher Training

Teachers are the navigators in this journey, and their readiness is crucial. Investing in comprehensive training programs that equip teachers with the knowledge and tools to integrate AI education effectively is non-negotiable. This training should go beyond the technical aspects, encompassing ethical considerations, societal impacts, and interdisciplinary applications of AI. Teachers should feel confident in delivering the content, sparking discussions, encouraging critical thinking, and guiding students in hands-on projects. Partnering with AI professionals and organizations for workshops or guest lectures can also provide fresh perspectives and keep the curriculum aligned with the latest developments in the field.

- Providing teachers with resources and training on AI education.
- Encouraging interdisciplinary teaching methods and critical discussions on AI.

- Facilitating partnerships with AI professionals to enhance learning.

Access to Resources

Equity in AI education is paramount. Every student deserves access to quality AI learning materials and opportunities regardless of background or location. This means ensuring schools everywhere have the necessary infrastructure, from internet access to computing hardware. Online platforms can play a significant role here, offering courses and resources students can access anywhere. However, it's also about creating opportunities for hands-on experience, whether through school labs, local maker spaces, or partnerships with tech companies. Scholarships and grants for underrepresented groups in tech can also help bridge the gap, ensuring a diverse future generation of AI innovators.

- Ensuring all schools have the necessary infrastructure for AI education.
- Leveraging online platforms to provide accessible AI learning resources.
- Creating opportunities for hands-on experience and supporting underrepresented groups.

Fostering Critical Thinking

Finally, and perhaps most importantly, education must aim to cultivate a generation of critical thinkers. AI's societal impacts are profound; understanding these implications is as crucial as mastering technology. The curriculum should encourage students to question, debate, and reflect on how AI is used, its benefits, and its challenges. Encouraging students to consider the ethical dimensions of AI, from privacy concerns to bias and inequality, prepares them not just as future technologists but as informed citizens. This holistic approach ensures that, as AI continues to shape our world, we have a populace equipped to use it wisely and ethically.

- Incorporating discussions on AI's ethical and societal impacts into the curriculum.
- Encouraging students to question and critically analyze AI applications.
- Preparing students to navigate the ethical complexities of AI as both technologists and citizens.

In this shifting educational paradigm, the goal is clear: to mold a future where every individual is not only aware of AI and its potential. Still, it is prepared to contribute to, critique, and ethically shape this technology's trajectory. This endeavor starts in the classroom but extends far beyond, promising a future enriched by AI, guided by well-informed, critically thinking citizens ready to tackle challenges and opportunities.

Ethical Considerations for Future AI Innovations

Navigating the terrain of AI innovation requires more than technical understanding; it also calls for a moral compass. The exhilarating pace at which AI is evolving brings to light ethical dilemmas that need addressing. It's not merely about avoiding pitfalls but actively cultivating a tech landscape where ethics guide innovation, ensuring technology serves humanity positively.

Ongoing Ethical Dialogue

The rapid growth of AI technologies makes it clear that ethics can't be one-off discussions. They must be as dynamic as the technology, evolving with each development. A continuous ethical dialogue ensures that as AI technologies advance, so does our understanding of their impact. This conversation isn't just for the philosophers or the tech gurus; it's a community-wide discussion that invites input from all sectors of society. Creating platforms where these discussions can thrive, from online forums to international conferences, is crucial. It's about keeping the conversation alive, ensuring it's inclusive, and making it actionable.

- Regularly updated forums and think tanks on AI ethics.
- Ethical discussions should be included in AI conferences and symposiums.
- Creation of accessible content that demystifies AI ethics for the general public.

Inclusion in AI Development

The beauty of diversity in AI development is not just a matter of fairness; it's a necessity for creating ethical AI systems. When a wide array of perspectives informs the development of AI technologies, the outcome is more likely to consider the needs and rights of a broader population segment. This inclusion means actively inviting voices from different genders, races, cultures, and socioeconomic backgrounds into the AI development process. By doing this, we can reduce biases and create AI technologies that truly understand and meet the diverse needs of people worldwide.

- Programs and initiatives to encourage underrepresented groups into AI fields.
- Diverse teams for AI project development and review processes.
- Collaborations between AI developers and community representatives.

Transparency in AI

Transparency in AI algorithms, data usage, and decision-making processes is not just about building trust; it's the foundation for accountability. When AI systems make decisions that affect lives—from loan approvals to medical diagnoses—understanding the "how" and "why" behind these decisions is paramount. This transparency allows for scrutiny, ensuring that AI systems are fair and just. Implementing measures like open-source AI models or transparent data policies helps peel back the layers of AI operations, making decisions more transparent. Moreover, clear documentation and communication about AI systems' functionality and limitations empower users, offering them insights into the technology that plays a significant role in their lives.

- Open-source AI models for public scrutiny and improvement.
- Clear and accessible data policies and AI system documentation.
- Regular audits of AI systems for transparency and fairness.

Global Cooperation

In the world of AI, no country stands alone. The digital world has no borders, and AI technologies developed anywhere can impact people everywhere. Therefore, establishing ethical norms and regulations for AI is a task that requires global cooperation. This collaboration ensures that moral standards have a universal foundation, preventing a scenario where AI ethics vary wildly from one country to another. International agreements on AI ethics can pave the way for global standards, fostering an environment where AI innovations respect human dignity and rights, regardless of where they are developed or deployed.

- International forums and task forces dedicated to AI ethics.
- Global agreements on baseline ethical standards for AI.
- Shared repositories of ethical AI resources and best practices.

In the future of AI, ethical considerations will be the key elements that will keep everything together. They ensure that as we develop new AI innovations, these advancements enhance our shared human values instead of compromising them. From fostering ongoing ethical dialogues and embracing inclusion in AI development to championing transparency and rallying for global cooperation, the path to ethical AI is paved with intention and collective action. It's a path that leads us toward a future where AI not only pushes the boundaries of what's possible but does so with a profound respect for the ethical implications of its advancement.

Community and Societal Engagement with AI

When we think about AI, it's easy to picture labs and tech companies as the main stages where the future is being written. Yet, the true essence of AI's transformative power lies within our communities and people's everyday lives. AI finds its most profound purpose in the interplay between technology and society here. This section explores how fostering a deeper connection between AI and communities can lead to more inclusive, impactful, and ethical technological advancements.

Public Awareness Campaigns

To truly integrate AI into the fabric of society, we need to start with awareness. Public awareness campaigns are pivotal in demystifying AI, highlighting its potential benefits and challenges. These campaigns can take various forms, from social media blitzes and informational websites to interactive exhibits in public spaces. The goal is to move beyond the buzzwords and showcase real-world applications of AI that touch on everyday life, such as innovative city initiatives, AI in healthcare, and the role of AI in environmental conservation. Equally important is addressing concerns head-on, providing clear, balanced information about job displacement, privacy issues, and ethical considerations, thereby fostering a well-informed public discourse around AI.

- Hosting AI demo days in community centers where locals can interact with AI technologies.
- Partnering with local media to produce feature stories on how AI is being used to solve community-specific problems.

Community AI Projects

Imagine harnessing a community's collective creativity and local knowledge to tackle issues they face, using AI as a tool. Community-led AI projects can address many challenges, from optimizing local traffic flow and reducing waste to enhancing public safety and supporting local businesses. By involving community members in the creativity and development process, these projects yield solutions tailored to local needs and cultivate a sense of ownership and understanding of AI technology. Schools, libraries, and local tech hubs can serve as incubators for these projects, providing resources, mentorship, and a platform for sharing outcomes.

- A city-wide challenge where teams develop AI solutions for efficient resource distribution to needy areas.
- A collaboration between local farmers and AI experts to create precision agriculture tools that maximize yield while conserving water.

Ethical AI Advocacy

Ensuring its ethical use is paramount as AI becomes more embedded in our lives. Community groups advocating for ethical AI practices and policies can serve as watchdogs and educators, bridging the gap between tech developers, policymakers, and the public. These groups can organize workshops, talks, and debates on ethical AI, creating forums for discussion and learning. They can also work closely with local governments and organizations to influence AI policy, ensuring it aligns with community values and ethical standards. By fostering a culture of ethical AI from the ground up, these groups help ensure that technological advancements benefit the many, not just the few.

- Formation of local ethics in AI discussion groups that meet regularly to dissect recent developments in AI technologies.
- Develop and disseminate a community AI ethics charter that outlines principles for responsible AI use within the community.

Participation in Policy Making

The trajectory of AI development should not be dictated solely by those who build or invest in AI technologies; the voices of those who live with the outcomes of these technologies are equally important. Encouraging community participation in AI policy-making ensures that diverse perspectives are considered, leading to more inclusive and effective policies. This can be facilitated through public consultations, participation in AI governance forums, and direct channels for feedback on AI initiatives. By actively involving community members in shaping AI policies, we reinforce the principle that AI should serve the public interest, aligning its development with the needs and values of society.

- Collaborate in workshops between policymakers, AI developers, and community members to draft AI guidelines for local government use.
- Online platforms where citizens can submit proposals and feedback on AI-related policies.

The fabric of our future, woven with threads of AI, will be more prosperous and more robust when all members of society share the loom. Through public awareness, community projects, ethical advocacy, and participatory policy-making, we can ensure AI evolves to respect our diverse needs, values, and aspirations. These initiatives foster a deeper understanding and acceptance of AI within communities and ensure that the development of AI technologies is guided by a broad spectrum of perspectives, leading to innovations that are beneficial, inclusive, and aligned with the public good.

Embracing AI: A Call to Action for Everyone

In a world swiftly reshaped by the winds of AI, each of us has the responsibility to stay informed and engaged. It's not just about keeping pace with technology but actively shaping its trajectory to ensure it enriches our lives and society. This section invites you to take up the mantle in the AI era, advocating for a proactive stance toward learning, engagement, and ethical considerations.

Personal Responsibility

The first step toward a harmonious future with AI is personal accountability in education. Understanding AI and its societal impacts does more than satisfy curiosity—it equips you with the knowledge to make informed decisions and contributions. This doesn't mean you need to become an AI expert overnight. Instead, it's about cultivating a habit of curiosity. Please start with the basics: what AI is, how it works, and its potential impact on society. From there, explore how AI is used daily and in the broader world. This foundational knowledge acts as your compass, guiding you through the complex landscape of AI.

- Start with AI literacy: familiarize yourself with AI concepts through articles, podcasts, and videos.
- Reflect on AI's role in your life and its broader societal impacts.

Proactive Engagement

Next, dive into the waters of proactive engagement with AI. This means moving beyond passive observation to active participation. Whether learning to code, joining AI-related discussions, or experimenting with AI tools, your engagement shapes your understanding and influences AI's development. Suppose coding isn't your cup of tea; worry not. Participation can take many forms, from contributing to AI discussions in online forums to attending AI-related events in your community. No matter how small, each action contributes to a more extensive understanding and dialogue around AI.

- Engage with AI tools: experiment with AI applications relevant to your interests or field.

- Join the conversation by participating in forums, attending workshops, and sharing your insights on AI's societal role.

Supporting Ethical AI Development

Supporting ethical AI development is crucial. It's about championing companies and organizations prioritizing transparency, fairness, and responsibility in their AI initiatives. Your support can manifest in various ways, from the products you buy to the projects you decide to back. Look for organizations that are open about their AI practices, commit to reducing biases in their AI systems, and actively consider the societal impacts of their technologies. By aligning your support with ethical AI practices, you contribute to a market that values and promotes responsible AI development.

- Research before you support: learn about companies' AI ethics policies and practices.
- Advocate for ethical AI: use your voice and platform to highlight the importance of ethical AI development.

Vision for a Collaborative Future

Envision a future where humans and AI work hand in hand, tackling some of the most pressing challenges we face. AI amplifies human capabilities in the future, allowing us to achieve more together than we ever could apart. From combating climate change to advancing medical research, the potential for positive impact is boundless. But realizing this vision requires more than technology—it demands collaboration, ethical consideration, and a commitment to using AI for the greater good. It's a call to action for everyone, from developers and policymakers to educators and citizens, to contribute their unique perspectives and skills toward building this future.

- Imagine the possibilities: consider how AI can address challenges in your community and beyond.
- Collaborate for impact: seek opportunities to work alongside AI developers, researchers, and other stakeholders on projects that leverage AI for positive societal change.

In wrapping up, this chapter has laid out the steps for embracing AI in our lives and society. The path forward is clear, from taking personal responsibility for AI education to engaging actively with AI technologies and supporting ethical development. The potential for AI to serve as a force for good in our world is immense, but realizing this potential requires effort from all of us. As we move into the next chapter, remember that the future of AI is not just something that happens to us—it's something we actively create together.

Afterword

Hey there, fellow AI adventurers!

We've come a long way together, haven't we? From those tentative steps into the world of Generative AI to now, where you're practically buzzing with all the cool stuff we've uncovered. This journey has been as eye-opening for you as when I first dipped my toes into these waters. Together, we've peeled back the layers of complexity around Generative AI, transforming it from a concept that might have once seemed as mystifying as quantum physics into a vibrant, accessible tool brimming with potential.

Remember how we started with the basics, building up your understanding piece by piece? And then, before you knew it, we were diving into real-world applications, from art to healthcare, and tackling those all-important ethical considerations. It's been quite the ride, showcasing not just how Generative AI can shape industries but how it's reshaping our approach to creativity, problem-solving, and innovation.

One of the big takeaways I hope you've gathered is the sheer scope of Generative AI's capabilities. But even more than that, its ethical use, the importance of staying on your toes with continuous learning, and adapting to an AI-driven future is key. AI isn't static; it's as dynamic as the world around us, constantly evolving, surprising, and challenging us to keep up.

Reflecting on our journey, I hope you've seen the shift in how you view AI. What might have once seemed like a distant, complex technology is now a tangible, powerful tool at your fingertips, ready to boost your personal and professional life into new realms of possibility.

Let's not forget about ethics—the backbone of responsible AI development and application. We've talked about the need for ongoing dialogue, inclusivity, and transparency to ensure AI doesn't just serve the few but benefits all of society. It's on us to keep these conversations alive and kicking.

Now, for the part where you come in—your call to action. Dive deeper into Generative AI, get your hands dirty with some tools, and join the discussions shaping the future of this technology. Don't just be a bystander; be a part of the movement steering AI towards a future we can all be proud of.

Supporting ethical AI development isn't just a nice-to-have; it's a must-do. Your voice and choices can influence a future where AI is used responsibly, ethically, and for the greater good. Remember, coders and tech moguls don't just write the future of AI; we all write it.

Imagine a future where humans and AI collaborate seamlessly, solving the grand challenges of our time, unlocking new avenues of creativity, and making our world more efficient and sustainable. That's the vision I'm inviting you to help create—a future not of humans vs. AI but humans with AI, working together in harmony.

As we wrap up this journey, I want to share a bit of my heart with you. When I first started exploring Generative AI, I felt excitement and trepidation, much like setting off on a grand adventure without a map. But look at us now – we've navigated this terrain together, and I'm filled with hope and anticipation for where we'll go next. My deepest wish is that this book has served as a valuable guide on your AI exploration journey and sparked a flame of curiosity within you. Stay curious, keep learning, and let's all play our part in shaping an AI-enhanced future as bright and inclusive as possible.

Let's not just ride the wave of AI innovation; let's steer it towards shores of unimaginable potential.

Here's to our shared future,

Gwen Taylor

Keeping the Game Alive

Wow, we've done it! Together, we've journeyed through the exciting world of Generative AI, turning complex concepts into clear insights. Now, you're equipped with everything you need to dive deeper into AI, ready to explore, create, and innovate. But guess what? The adventure doesn't have to end here.

Your new understanding can light the way for others just starting, curious and eager to learn like you were. By sharing your thoughts about this book on Amazon, you can help guide them. Your review is more than just your opinion; it's a beacon for fellow tech enthusiasts searching for a clear and friendly introduction to Generative AI.

Leaving a review is easy and quick, but it makes a real difference. It helps others discover this guide, sparking their interest in AI and supporting them as they start their journey. Your feedback keeps the spirit of learning and discovery alive, ensuring that the fascinating world of AI continues to grow and inspire.

Scan the QR code below and share your journey:

Thank you so much for your support. By sharing your experience, you're not just helping keep the game of learning AI alive; you're an essential part of a community that values knowledge, curiosity, and growth. Let's continue to explore the possibilities of Generative AI together, armed with the knowledge we've shared and the discoveries still to come.

Thank you for being a pivotal part of this learning journey. Here's to many more adventures in the ever-evolving world of AI!

Bibliography

11 Best Generative AI Tools and Platforms in 2024 https://www.turing.com/resources/generative-ai-tools

12 Data Science & AI Competitions to Advance Your Skills ... https://towardstowarddatascience.com/12-data-science-ai-competitions-to-advance-your-skills-in-2021-32e3fcb95d8c

4 Ways AI Transformed Music, Movies, and Art in 2023 https://time.com/6343945/ai-music-movies-art-2023/

7 Best Artificial Intelligence Courses to Learn AI in 2024 https://www.learndatasci.com/best-artificial-intelligence-ai-courses/

A Practical Guide to Building Ethical AI https://hbr.org/2020/10/a-practical-guide-to-building-ethical-ai

AI in Supply Chain Management: Use Cases, Impact, & More https://flow.space/blog/ai-in-supply-chain/

AI Is Deepening the Digital Divide - InformationWeek https://www.informationweek.com/machine-learning-ai/ai-is-deepening-the-digital-divide

Artificial Intelligence regulation, global trends https://www.ey.com/en_cn/ai/how-to-navigate-global-trends-in-artificial-intelligence-regulation

DALL·E: Creating images from text https://openai.com/research/dall-e

Deep Learning vs. Machine Learning: A Beginner's Guide https://www.coursera.org/articles/ai-vs-deep-learning-vs-machine-learning-beginners-guide#:~:text=In%20short%2C%20machine%20learning%20is,process%20of%20the%20human%20brain

Economic potential of generative AI https://www.mckinsey.com/capabilities/mckinsey-digital/our-insights/the-economic-potential-of-generative-ai-the-next-productivity-frontier

Ethical concerns mount as AI takes bigger decision-making role https://news.harvard.edu/gazette/story/2020/10/ethical-concerns-mount-as-ai-takes-bigger-decision-making-role/

Ethics of Artificial Intelligence https://www.unesco.org/en/artificial-intelligence/recommendation-ethics

Generative AI and the future of work in America https://www.mckinsey.com/mgi/our-research/generative-ai-and-the-future-of-work-in-america

Generative AI Ethics: 8 Biggest Concerns and Risks https://www.techtarget.com/searchenterpriseai/tip/Generative-AI-ethics-8-biggest-concerns

How AI Advertising Drives More Effective Marketing ... https://www.invoca.com/blog/ai-advertising-effective-campaigns

How AI Can Help Cut Energy Costs While Meeting Ambitious ESG Goals https://hbr.org/sponsored/2023/09/how-ai-can-help-cut-energy-costs-while-meeting-ambitious-esg-goals

How AI Could Bring Big Changes to Education https://www.edsurge.com/news/2023-11-14-how-ai-could-bring-big-changes-to-education-and-how-to-avoid-worst-case-scenarios

How AI is transforming the creative economy and music industry https://www.ohio.edu/news/2024/01/how-ai-transforming-creative-economy-and-music-industry

How Generative AI Is Already Transforming Customer ... https://www.bcg.com/publications/2023/how-generative-ai-transforms-customer-service

How to leverage AI in community engagement https://www.citizenlab.co/blog/civic-engagement/how-to-leverage-ai-in-community-engagement%EF%BF%BC/

How to Use Chat GPT? A Simple Guide for Beginners https://www.analyticsvidhya.com/blog/2023/05/how-to-harness-the-full-potential-of-chatgpt-tips-prompts/

Human values in the loop: Design principles for ethical AI https://www2.deloitte.com/us/en/insights/focus/cognitive-technologies/design-principles-ethical-artificial-intelligence.html

Leading smart home trends worldwide 2023 | Statista https://www.statista.com/statistics/1374564/smart-home-trends/

Machine Learning for Beginners: An Introduction to Neural Networks https://towardstowarddatascience.com/machine-learning-for-beginners-an-introduction-to-neural-networks-d49f22d238f9

Privacy in the age of generative AI https://stackoverflow.blog/2023/10/23/privacy-in-the-age-of-generative-ai/

Revolutionizing healthcare: the role of artificial intelligence in ... https://bmcmededuc.biomedcentral.com/articles/10.1186/s12909-023-04698-z

Space and Generative AI: Believe the Hype https://www.kratosdefense.com/constellations/articles/space-and-generative-ai-believe-the-hype

The 10 Best AI Writers & Content Generators Compared https://www.searchenginejournal.com/ai-writers-content-generators/448782/

The AI–quantum computing mash-up: will it revolutionize ... https://www.nature.com/articles/d41586-023-04007-0

The History of Artificial Intelligence: Complete AI Timeline https://www.techtarget.com/searchenterpriseai/tip/The-history-of-artificial-intelligence-Complete-AI-timeline

The History of Artificial Intelligence: Complete AI Timeline https://www.techtarget.com/searchenterpriseai/tip/The-history-of-artificial-intelligence-Complete-AI-timeline

The Impact of the GDPR on Artificial Intelligence - Securiti.ai https://securiti.ai/impact-of-the-gdpr-on-artificial-intelligence/

The rise of generative AI: A timeline of breakthrough innovations https://www.qualcomm.com/news/onq/2024/02/the-rise-of-generative-ai-timeline-of-breakthrough-innovations#:~:text=Breakthroughs%20in%20generative%20models,engages%20two%20competing%20neural%20networks

The state of AI in 2023: Generative AI's breakout year https://www.mckinsey.com/capabilities/quantumblack/our-insights/the-state-of-ai-in-2023-generative-ais-breakout-year

Top Generative AI Use Cases and Applications https://www.xenonstack.com/blog/generative-ai-use-cases

What Do We Do About the Biases in AI? https://hbr.org/2019/10/what-do-we-do-about-the-biases-in-ai

Why A Growth Mindset Is Essential For Career Success https://www.forbes.com/sites/carolinecastrillon/2019/07/09/why-a-growth-mindset-is-essential-for-career-success/

Why Community Engagement is Imperative for AI Success https://www.conference-board.org/brief/marketing-communications/Community-Engagement-Imperative-for-AI-Success

Made in the USA
Coppell, TX
23 September 2024

37555957R00105